Peace
Within
Yourself

Peace Within Yourself

The Meaning of The Book of John

Joseph Murphy
Ph.D., D.D.

Published 2019 by Gildan Media LLC
aka G&D Media
www.GanddMedia.com

Design by Meghan Day Healey of Story Horse, LLC

Library of Congress Cataloging-in-Publication Data is available upon request

ISBN: 978-1-7225-0134-1

10   9   8   7   6   5   4   3   2   1

Contents

Introduction

This book is based on a series of lectures and classes given on the inner meaning of the *Book of John* in America and many other parts of the world. In 1948 I published *St. John Speaks* giving the psychological life-germ hidden behind the words of this book. It was very popular and became a transforming instrument lifting the minds of students from the literal to a higher level of meaning. Due to innumerable requests all over the world, I have issued this revised, enlarged edition giving the essence of my most popular of all lectures on the *Book of John*.

The Bible is a book intended to teach you correct mental and spiritual processes. The object of all the Bible parables, allegories, and discourses is to convey spiritual truth so that man may learn to advance and grow spiritually. In a series of lectures on the spiritual meaning behind the stories in the *Book of John* in South Africa, Japan, India, and Europe on a recent world lecture tour, I said to thousands of students, "Unless you have the inner psychological and spiritual meaning behind the Bible, you have no Bible at all." Paul said, "For the letter killeth, but the spirit giveth life." 2 COR. 3:6.

The Bible contains the congealed wisdom of the ages. A holy man in India said to me last year that the *Book of John* was the most mystical of all books of the Bible or any Bible in the world. He added that it was the most profound work on the laws of life.

The ancient writers of the Bible were illumined men; they had three ways of expressing their thoughts. The same word took in their pleasures—the literal, figurative, and the hieroglyphic sense. The first two ways, that is to say, those which consisted of taking words in the literal or figurative sense, were spoken; but the third which could only receive its hieroglyphic form by means of the characters of which the words were composed, existed only for the eyes and was used only in writing. (See *The Hebraic Tongue Restored*, Fabre D'Olivet.) Through an understanding of the symbols and the meaning of each Hebrew letter (denoting a certain state of consciousness), man can interpret the Bible without much difficulty. Strong's *Concordance* and Young's *Concordance* are used by the writer in determining the meaning of names in the Bible.

Truth comes as a sword, for we must die to our illusions (beliefs in merely historical Biblical characters) and awaken to the psychological significance before man can know himself. The Bible is essentially a story about ourselves although undoubtedly some of the characters were factually historical. All the stories in the Bible teach functional psychology and practical metaphysics. Any of the historical characters, therefore, refer to attained levels of consciousness—moods, feelings, and ideas. The carnal mind (conscious mind, the intellect) has difficulty in grasping the things of the spirit. This is the reason so many students of New Thought do not grow faster spiritually. They will cling fanatically to historical characters as such and fail to secure confidence in themselves—in their Self—The One Altogether Lovely! They are so busy setting up outer gods that they ignore the God within.

We get nowhere in the New Thought Movement by attacking the historicity of Jesus, Moses, Paul, etc; all this is idle speculation and a waste of time. Why not accept "the bare bones" of historical fact (not ecclesiastical jargon and legend), and begin clothing the bones with the flesh and blood of metaphysical reality and wisdom? The writer believes there was a man called Jesus who lived and performed so-called miracles of healing, but the historical Jesus also symbolizes and personifies the Universal Principle common to all individual men.

The Jesus of the Bible has more than one meaning. The word *Joshua* is identical with the name Jesus. Joshua (Jesus) means God is Savior. God is Deliverer. When you read the Bible, look upon Jesus as Taylor said, "illumined reason or your knowledge of God." It also means realization of your desire, the solution to your problem or salvation, the God-Presence within. Jesus symbolizes the cornerstone rejected, but which is most essential in building the temple of God-consciousness. The realization of our desire saves us from any predicament in the world; therefore, that is our savior. Our own consciousness or conviction saves us. "Thy faith hath made thee whole."

It is never a man that saves; it is that saving state of consciousness which works the miracle. A man with hatred in his heart finds love is his savior since it restores peace. Love would be Jesus—or savior—in that instance. The truth which Jesus taught saves, not the man Jesus. The man Jesus merely discovered the truth that functions in and about himself. "Ye shall know the truth, and the truth shall make you free." By example, your feelings or mood of opulence will save you from poverty.

Undoubtedly the great mystics who wrote the Bible used the historical Jesus as the ideal man whom every man aspires to be. They also used him to personify spiritual and ideal states of consciousness. Instead of worshiping men, let us increase the valuation we place upon ourselves. Instead of worshiping Jesus as God, let us find and worship the God of Jesus. Do not bow mentally to idols or strange gods, as your own awareness is God—the only Living Reality.

The Gospel according to St. John (*gospel*—good news)* should not be studied from the historical viewpoint. It teaches you how to bring health, harmony, and peace into your life by increased understanding of God. Let us be asleep to the world, awaken to God, and move upward from glory to glory walking always in the Light.

Jesus gave us the challenge, "Be ye perfect as the Father is." Does this not mean that as long as we persist in and remain on the human, conscious level, we can never cease being man? Hence we never become as God in our respective world of body, mind, and circumstance.

We must realize that God is Omnipresent. He is in us and He is the very life of us. He has His own Unity and Integrity in Himself, but you have Him in you on your level of awareness.

---

* All Bible references are from the *Book of John*, unless otherwise indicated.

Chapter 1

(1) *In the beginning was the Word, and the Word was with God, and the Word was God.*

In the beginning means the beginning of any creative process. Let us put the above quotation into application immediately. You read in the Bible, *He sent his word and healed them.* Suppose you wish to pray for your mother who is ill; you would send your word this way. The *word* means your desire, your clearly formulated idea or concept. Your desire or word must be specific and definite. You have the idea of perfect health for your mother. This idea is real. It is the seed which, as Troward says, has its own mathematics and mechanics with it. You don't give life to the seed; you can't make it grow. You deposit it in the soil, and by a process of watering and fertilizing the seed, you accelerate its growth; you don't coerce or make it grow. It has its own vitality and power to grow as inherent qualities.

The word was with God. This is your second step. *With* is a preposition joining two ideas together by feeling. The word *with* means feeling, conviction. As you still the wheels of your mind by thinking of the Healing Presence within which created your mother, your mind becomes receptive. This is the soil in which you deposit your seed or desire. Feel and know that the Healing Power of God is now transforming, healing, and restoring your mother into God's perfect pattern of harmony, health, and peace. Continue to do this until you get into the mental atmosphere or mood of health. You can even imagine your mother is home, doing the things she always did. You can hear her tell how the miracle of God worked in her life and her remarkable recovery. All this can be made intensely vivid and real in your Divine, mental workshop. Your feeling of health is now resurrected in the mind of your mother and releases its healing and therapeutic potency there. The reason for this is that there is only one mind, and in the mind-principle there is no time or space; hence your idea of perfect health is instantaneously felt by her. You are thinking of your mother which identifies her in Divine mind. She, being the receiving station, receives your heavenly broadcasts, as subjectively you are one; in the subjective, passive, receptive state of mind there is no here nor there. Your thought is Omnipresent.

You may continue to pray for your mother two or three times a day in the above manner, paying no attention whatsoever to hospital reports, or the belief or opinion of relatives. Continue to know that your thought and feeling are the *words* which heal. This is your authority. You are the mental surgeon performing a delicate, mental operation. Your instruments (thought and feeling) must be sterilized at all times. Incisively and decisively you reject all fearthoughts and you speak the word with conviction knowing that what you decree governs and controls your mother's body. You have succeeded in giving life to the concept of perfect health for your mother in your own mind, knowing the idea will germinate and grow of its own accord. You watered it with faith and expectancy, and your word (your inner feeling, your conviction of health) was God. It was good (God and good are synonymous). It came to birth as a perfect healing for the person you prayed for. You have put into application the formula of prayer.

The whole *Gospel of John* teaches how consciousness accepts an idea and projects it as a condition, experience, or event. This same idea is expressed in the story of the whale swallowing Jonah. The *whale* represents your subconscious mind which receives any idea (Jonah) felt as true; then expresses (or casts forth on dry land) what is impressed upon it.

It is said Jonah remained in the belly of the whale for three days. This represents the length of time it takes you to reach a conviction or the feeling your prayer is answered. It has nothing to do with three days time. The numeral *three* represents the length of time you work with the idea mentally, until it is absorbed by your consciousness.

(2) *The same was in the beginning with God.* (3) *All things were made by him; and without him was not any thing made that was made.* (4) *In him was life; and the life was the light of men.*

There is only One Creative Power. There is only One Source. God is called Awareness, Unconditioned Consciousness, Life. There is only one Life and all things in the world are made inside and out of Life or Consciousness. The Bible calls God I AM which means Being or Existence. I AM conceives itself to be sun, moon, stars, planets, etc. In fact, everything you see is the I AM in infinite differentiation. There is only one Cause, one Substance, one Source. Whatever you affix to I AM through feeling, you create in your world of expression. That is what the Bible means when it says that there is nothing made that is not made that way. Nothing is made without feeling. If you feel poor, you become poor; if you feel prosperous, you become prosperous; if you feel dignified, you become dignified.

Light means Intelligence in the Bible. Infinite Intelligence is within you (I AM). Feel and know that you are Divinely led in all your ways and that is exactly what you will experience; then you will know and feel the meaning of *and the life was the light of men.*

(5) *And the light shineth in darkness; and the darkness comprehended it not.* (6) *There was a man sent from God, whose name was John.* (7) *The same came for a witness, to bear witness of the Light, that all men through him might believe.*

Darkness refers to ignorance or lack of knowledge of the way our mind works. We are in darkness when we do not know that as we think and feel so are we. Man is a conditioned state of the Unconditioned One, with all the qualities, attributes, and potencies of God. Man is here to discover who he is. He is not an automaton. He has the capacity to think two ways—positively and negatively. When he begins to discover that the only good and evil he experiences are due to the action of his own mind, he begins to awaken from the sense of bondage and limitation to the outside world. Not knowing the laws of mind, man does not know how to bring forth his desire.

The name *John* does not refer to any particular man, but represents a state of consciousness where man begins to intellectually perceive the truth. All of us are here to bear witness of the Light (God) within. We bear true witness when we express harmony, health, and peace in our mind, body, and environment. Jesus is a symbol of every man continually transcending himself. He was called the Wayshower setting forth and revealing the powers within all men. He said to all, *"The things I do, ye shall do and even greater things shall ye do."*

The same Power which Jesus used is within all of us. If we will only rise in consciousness to the point of acceptance which Jesus did, we, too, will open the eyes of the blind, unstop the ears of the deaf, and do all the things which Jesus did because we believe.

(8) *He was not that Light, but was sent to bear witness of that Light. (9) That was the true Light, which lighteth every man that cometh into the world. (10) He was in the world, and the world was made by him, and the world knew him not. (11) He came unto his own, and his own received him not.*

Verse eight means your intellect (another name for John) is not the true light; it is a projection of the Infinite Intelligence within. But when my intellect is anointed or illumined by the Wisdom of God, I bear witness of the Light.

A simple illustration of this is as follows: I had a knotty problem to solve a few days ago before I started to write on this chapter. I got still, relaxed, and said, "Infinite Intelligence knows only the answer. The answer is mine now." I dismissed the matter and started writing. While writing these last few lines, the answer popped into my conscious mind like toast pops out of a toaster. This is called guidance or intuition. *Intuition* is simply the Wisdom of God lodged in the subjective of man, rising to the surface mind, revealing to man the solution or answer. We use the intellect (John) to carry out the inner dictates of the Divine Presence.

The true *light which lighteth every man* represents the I AM or God in man. In simple, every day language we say that awareness or consciousness is the light of the world. This is readily understood.

If, for example, you were not aware of something, it would not be in your world. Supposing a house fell down a few blocks away from you, if you did not see it happen or hear the noise, so far as you are concerned, it did not happen; your light (awareness) did not shine on it; therefore it is not a part of your consciousness. Remember this truth—Whatever you become aware of comes into your world. In other words, your awareness is the light which creates your world. By *your world* I mean your body, circumstances, environment, and all your experiences.

You have already read in verse five *the light shineth in darkness*. False concepts, wrong theories, and negative thoughts represent your darkness. If you believe a fan gives you a stiff neck, it is a false light or knowledge and causes suffering in your world. Ideas and concepts which inspire you, thoughts which elevate, dignify, heal, and bless you represent the Wisdom of God which is the true Light. True knowledge of God will light up the heaven of your mind and give you peace, serenity, a sense of security, and tranquillity. I believe you have a good idea of what the word *awareness* is all about now. We must remember that we create our own world after the image and likeness of our own mental pictures and thought patterns.

Verse ten points out that your consciousness is the creator of your world, but the majority of people do not know that the cause of all is their own state of consciousness. *A state of consciousness* means what you think, feel, believe, and mentally assent to.

Verse eleven explains that the average person refuses to believe that his state of consciousness is the cause of all his experiences—good or bad. He prefers to blame something outside himself.

(12) *But as many as received him, to them gave he power to become the sons of God, even to them that believe on his name.*

The same power which Jesus used is within all men. If we completely accepted the fact that God is Omnipotent in the same way that we make a telephone call, we could raise the dead, heal the blind, and do all the things which Jesus did. We, theoretically, give assent to these truths but we do not really believe them in our heart. This is why we keep on praying in order to convince ourselves of the truth which we affirm. As long as we go on believing we are sons of John Jones or Tom Thumb, we will never do the works of God. All we have to do is to recognize the Power of God and believe; then the miracle will happen.

(13) *Which were born, not of blood, nor of the will of the flesh, nor of the will of man, but of God.* (14) *And the Word was made flesh, and dwelt among us (and we beheld his glory, the glory as of the only begotten of the Father,) full of grace and truth.*

The *flesh and blood* spoken of represents our present limitations which pass away the minute we recognize the Spiritual Power within, realizing its Omnipotence, knowing at the same time it is responding to our thought-patterns and mental imagery. The *will of God* is the Nature of God; and the Nature of God is Goodness, Truth, Beauty, Wholeness, Completeness, and Perfection.

The words *being made flesh* is experienced by you when you enter into the feeling of being healed; then you will be healed. Thus the word (your desire) is made flesh (manifested), and you behold the glory (Divine idea objectified) of the only begotten (your supreme desire) full of grace and truth, meaning harmony and the happiness which follow your answered prayer.

(15) *John bare witness of him, and cried, saying, This was he of whom I Spake, He that cometh after me is preferred before me: for he was before me.* (16) *And of his fulness have all we received, and grace for grace.* (17) *For the law was given by Moses, but grace and truth came by Jesus Christ.*

You are John and you are always bearing witness or testifying to your state of consciousness. All external change follows inner change.

Dr. Nicoll, in his writings, speaks of the language of parables, allegories, and miracles of the Bible. What he is saying is that everything said in the Bible, whether parable, allegory, or discourse has a definite, inner, psychological meaning, apart from the literal sense.

Look at the statement, *"He that cometh after me is preferred before me."* The consciousness or conviction of being healed must precede the healing. There was a man with a paralyzed hand who healed himself recently (a member of our audience) by claiming ten or fifteen minutes several times daily that the Healing Power of God was healing, vitalizing, and restoring his hand. He became a new man. The man with the paralyzed hand died and the man with the perfect, functioning hand awakened. This refers to the death in the belief of paralysis and the birth of the idea of perfect health. It is your own consciousness dying to an old state and giving birth to the new concept.

Verse seventeen means the law and the word, the cosmic (Moses) and the personal (Jesus). Moses is your desire, and Jesus is your conviction. Moses and Jesus refer to two phases of your own consciousness. Moses gives us the law that feeling is the creator. Jesus Christ means the harmonious union or functioning of our conscious and subconscious mind. Christ is the fulfilling of the law. *Jesus Christ* in simple, everyday language means I am filled full of the feeling of being what I long to be. Grace and truth (love and freedom) follow that state of consciousness.

(18) *No man hath seen God at any time; the only begotten Son, which is in the bosom of the Father, he hath declared him.* (19) *And this is the record of John, when the Jews sent priests and Levites from Jerusalem to ask him, Who art thou?* (20) *And he confessed, and denied not; but confessed, I am not the Christ.* (21) *And they asked him, What then? Art thou Elias? And he saith, I am not. Art thou that prophet? And he answered, No.* (22) *Then said they unto him, Who art thou? that we may give an answer to them that sent us. What sayest thou of thyself?*

We do not see God with the naked eye. We see God in the same way that we see an answer to a knotty mathematical or geometrical problem. All men are begotten of the Only One. We are all sons or expressions of the One God or Life. Your clarified desire is also a son of God or idea of the Infinite. Your desire for health is a definite promise or declaration of the God-Power to heal you.

John (intellect) is not the Christ (Wisdom of God). Art thou Elias? Elias means God is Savior. Before the answer to any problem can come into our experience, we must realize that Infinite Intelligence is within and responds to our thought. In other words, Elias must come first. Art thou that prophet? The prophet is always Jesus or your inner conviction or feeling which determines what is to come. A simple way of answering the above Bible verse fifteen is to realize *John* is your conscious mind awakening to the truth. *Christ* is the subjective Wisdom and Power of God which you call forth when you still your mind and reject the appearance of things. As you quietly contemplate the answer, you become aware of the Inner Voice and Divine Wisdom which wells up and anoints your intellect showing you the way you should go.

(23) *He said, I am the voice of one crying in the wilderness, Make straight the way of the Lord, as said the prophet Esaias. (24) And they which were sent were of the Pharisees. (25) And they asked him, and said unto him, Why baptizest thou then, if thou be not that Christ, nor Elias, neither that prophet? (26) John answered*

them, saying, I baptize with water: but there standeth one among you, whom ye know not.

The voice crying in the wilderness is the cosmic urge, the ideals, and impulses which well up in all of us. It is the innate Principle of Life or God in all of us which ever seeks to do right. It is like a voice in the wilderness crying for the right way. When we are *in the wilderness*, we are in a limited state. The Lord is the power and the authority of our mind in tune with the Infinite. We are in the wilderness of hearsay, idle thought, and opinion until we awaken to the Kingdom of God within. This kingdom is not afar off in time or space but co-exists with the life of all of us. We can enter into the kingdom of peace, harmony, and joy when we cleanse our mind of false beliefs (baptism) and accept the Truths of God. John (conscious mind) baptizes with water. We are not, of course, cleansed by pouring water on the head. We have only to *cleanse our feet and we are clean every whit whole.*

The *feet* symbolize our understanding. When we die to our false beliefs and superstitions, we are ready to believe that the God-Presence is none other than our consciousness or awareness. Our consciousness is without face, form, or figure. It is the Invisible, Formless Power within us taking form according to our thought and feeling. Here in your world of the mind or consciousness, you are the Christ or King of your world. Your *robe* as a king is the garment or mood of love. The *crown* you wear is the awareness of the Power of God. The *scepter* you hold is your authority to use this Power to bless, heal, and inspire.

John said, *I baptize thee with water.* Water, of course, is used here in a special sense. Jesus said, *The water that I shall give him shall be in him a well of water springing up into everlasting life.* JOHN 4:14.

Water means Truth or the Wisdom of God reigning supreme in the mind of man. As you read these words, you know the power of your own thoughts to take charge of your mind, expel all enemies, and direct the Divine forces wisely and constructively. *The poor and the needy seek water and there is none, and their tongue faileth for thirst.* ISAIAH 41:17. Suppose you baptize yourself with water now. Water means your consciousness which, like water, will assume the shape of any vessel into which it is poured. The vessel is your mental attitude or your feeling. Our unconditioned consciousness is always conditioned (conditions, experiences, and events in our life) by what we think, feel, and believe. To know this is to possess the truth which liberates you. It certainly baptizes or cleanses the mind of beliefs in external powers and causes. Our feeling of health produces health; our feeling of wealth produces wealth.

(27) *He it is, who coming after me is preferred before me, whose shoe's latchet I am not worthy to unloose. (28) These things were done in Bethabara beyond Jordan, where John was baptizing. (29) The next day John seeth Jesus coming unto him, and saith, Behold the Lamb of God, which taketh away the sin of the world.*

In verse twenty-seven we are told that the conscious mind is not worthy to unloose the latchet of the shoes of the deeper mind or subjective self. By the *subjective self* I mean not just the subconscious mind, but the Presence of God or the I AM within us. *Feet* symbolize understanding, and the shoes cover the feet. In other words the conscious mind does not know the secret of creation or the manner in which the Infinite Wisdom and Intelligence within man brings things to pass. Its ways are past finding out. The conscious mind cannot unlock or reveal how, when, where, or through what source the answer to prayer will come. Many things seem impossible to the conscious mind, but to the Invisible Power within man, all things are possible. *Canst thou believe? All things are possible to him that believeth.*

In verse twenty-nine the *Lamb of God* is a symbolic reference to the sun as it enters the sign of Aries, a ram or a lamb. The ancients called the sun the savior of the world as it redeems the world from darkness and death when it ascends the heavens. When John (your intellect) recognizes Jesus (the God-Power within), you begin to fulfill your desires and aspirations, and your sins (your failure to reach your goal and fulfill your desires) are taken away.

(30) *This is he of whom I said, After me cometh a man which is preferred before me: for he was before me. (31) And I knew him not: but that he should be made manifest to Israel, therefore am I come baptizing with water. (32) And John bare record, saying, I saw the Spirit descending from heaven like a dove, and it abode upon him. (33) And I knew him not: but he that sent me to baptize with water, the same said unto me, Upon whom thou shalt see the Spirit descending, and remaining on him, the same is he which baptizeth with the Holy Ghost. (34) And I saw, and bare record that this is the Son of God. (35) Again the next day after John stood, and two of his disciples; (36) And looking upon Jesus as he walked, he saith, Behold the Lamb of God! (37) And the two disciples heard him speak, and they followed Jesus. (38) Then Jesus turned, and saw them following, and saith unto them, What seek ye? They said unto him, Rabbi (which is to say, being interpreted, Master), where dwellest thou? (39) He saith unto them, Come and see. They came and saw where he dwelt, and abode with him that day: for it was about the tenth hour. (40) One of the two which heard John speak, and followed him, was Andrew, Simon Peter's*

brother. (41) He first findeth his own brother Simon, and saith unto him, We have found the Messias, which is, being interpreted, the Christ. (42) And he brought him to Jesus. And when Jesus beheld him, he said, Thou art Simon the son of Jona: thou shalt be called Cephas, which is by interpretation, A stone (43) The day following Jesus would go forth into Galilee, and findeth Philip, and saith unto him, Follow me. (44) Now Philip was of Bethsaida, the city of Andrew and Peter. (45) Philip findeth Nathanael, and saith unto him, We have found him, of whom Moses in the law, and the prophets, did write, Jesus of Nazareth, the son of Joseph. (46) And Nathanael said unto him, Can there any good thing come out of Nazareth? Philip saith unto him, Come and see. (47) Jesus saw Nathanael coming to him, and saith of him, Behold an Israelite indeed in whom is no guile! (48) Nathanael saith unto him, whence knowest thou me? Jesus answered and said unto him, Before that Philip called thee, when thou wast under the fig tree, I saw thee. (49) Nathanael answered and saith unto him, Rabbi, thou art the Son of God; thou art the King of Israel. (50) Jesus answered and said unto him, Because I said unto thee, I saw thee under the fig tree, believest thou? thou shalt see greater things than these. (51) And he saith unto him, Verily, verily, I say unto you, Hereafter ye shall see heaven open, and the angels ascending and descending upon the Son of man.

The essence of the above verses is a wonderful formula for prayer, its meaning is as follows: In verse thirty-eight the question, *Where dwellest thou?* obviously does not refer to a village or a street address. To think so would be too absurd for words. It means, where do you dwell in consciousness—your state of mind? Do you abide in the consciousness of love and oneness with God? We must so discipline our minds that we remain unmoved and impervious to the negation of the world. The disciples Andrew, Simon, Philip, and Nathanael represent faculties and powers within us. Jesus represents our I AM or Consciousness. Andrew means perception, i.e., seeing the truth about anything. You are using the disciple or faculty Andrew when you know God has the answer, that there is a way out, and when contemplating the happy ending. Simon means to hear the good news. You are using this faculty when you no longer look to outer conditions for hope or encouragement.

In verse forty-two Simon's name is changed to a stone. A stone means the rock of faith. A *stone* is hard, solid, and fixed. This means your faith is immovable and unshakeable. Now your confidence is trust in the Invisible Spirit within which becomes all things to all men. Your knowledge of the law enables you to maintain a strong conviction regardless of appearances and outer change.

The next faculty you call is *Philip* which means perseverance and stick-to-it-ive-ness. Philip means a lover of horses. A trainer of horses is firm but kind. He has the rare quality of patience, perseverance, and determination. You need these qualities to succeed in prayer-life also. Many people quit after a few days and say, "What's the use? It doesn't work for me." Be Philip and ride your horse (mood) to victory. Keep your attention focused on your goal by frequent occupancy of the mind until it takes root within you; then you are using Philip's qualities of character and action.

Philip finds Nathanael—the latter meaning the gift of God (our desire). In verse forty-five we read, *We have found him of whom Moses in the law, and the prophets, did write, Jesus of Nazareth, the son of Joseph. Joseph* means disciplined imagination. *Jesus* is our solution to that which we want, and it comes from Nazareth (a stem, sprout, idea, thought). If we will take that sprout or idea, no matter how fantastic it is, and see it clearly as a fact now existing in consciousness, we have psychologically called *Andrew*. If we will have faith in God to bring it to pass, we have called *Simon* (the faculty of hearing or feeling the good tidings within). We sustain or ride that mood until it becomes a subjective embodiment within us. We are now calling Philip. Then *Nathanael* appears (the gift of God—our desire made manifest). We say, "Yes, this is Jesus (my answered prayer, my solution) and He is of Nazareth (that idea or desire I nourished). Yea, verily, it is the son of Joseph, the manifestation of what I imagined and felt subjectively as true." When we completely accept our desire in consciousness without reservations, we are, indeed, an Israelite without guile.

Verse forty-eight speaks of a *fig tree* meaning we are in a state of sorrow, sadness, and limitation until we discover our Inner Power. When we call our three disciples, we come out of the limitation and no longer sit under the fig tree of lack. Our own consciousness i.e., thought and feeling, possess the answer to our need, did we but know where and how to seek and find it. The metaphysical key to demonstration is offered in the following statement: Before we ever pray for anything, "It is." Creation is finished. We simply give expression to that which has already been formed subjectively and spiritually.

Go within now; claim, feel, and imagine what you want in a meditative state and become one with it. I do not know how often you will have to do this, but this I do know, if you will continue to remain faithful to your mental picture, the Almighty Power will objectify your ideal. Whatever you envision, you can achieve. Do not fail to dream lofty dreams (angels of God ascending and descending) and make them come true. In moments of meditation, as you get lost in the joy of being what you long to be, you are ascending with your ideal to the heavens of your own mind. In a little while you will see it descend on the objective plane as a condition, experience, or event. The practice of these simple truths is *the true light which lighteth every man that cometh into the world.*

Chapter 2

The first miracle by Jesus is recorded here as that of changing water into wine. We discover about one thousand years previously that the same story is recorded of Bacchus, the wine God. The cup spoken of in the New Testament and the chalice of Bacchus are identical in meaning. The ancients called the juice of the grapes the blood of Bacchus. All this is symbolic and is merely telling us that by the transformation of our consciousness, we can realize our desire. *Changing water into wine* means experiencing the joy of the answered prayer.

The consciousness of health produces health. The consciousness or feeling of wealth, produces wealth. Consciousness is all things to all men, and whatever you assume yourself to be, you experience. In the same manner as you press juice out of a grape, so do you press out of your consciousness all things you wish by assuming you are what you long to be. As you live in the mental atmosphere of being what you long to be, that mental atmosphere becomes saturated, and like saturated clouds fall as rain, so will there be a precipitation of your good on the screen of space.

Bacchus was depicted as the god of good-cheer and hilarity. The poets have been rather eloquent in the praise of this mythological character. The names Bacchus, Osiris, Dionysus, Chrishna, and Adonis which signify the Lord of Heaven or the Lord and God of Light are all terms referring to a God-Presence within. The above names are masks of concealed truth. In the Greek ceremonies, pots of water were carried into the temple and placed at the feet of god. It was reported that overnight the water changed to wine. This so-called wine was then distributed to the multitude and referred to as the blood of Bacchus. The *wine*, of course, refers to spiritual food, or the Wisdom of God.

The *marriage feast* is the union of the mind with Divine Wisdom. The *Rubaiyat* of Omar Khayyam refers to the feast of bread and wine, the same eternal story of man's feasting on the Wisdom, Truth, and Beauty referred to as the bread of God. *Drinking the Wine* is the inspiration, joy, and love which well up in man as he animates and makes alive God's Truths in his heart. An inner transformation takes place, and he becomes a new man, because he drank of the new wine* or the new interpretation of life.

Prayer is likened in the Bible to a wedding feast. The Kingdom of Heaven is within. In the unconscious depths of man is to be found the Infinite Intelligence, Power, and Love of the Infinite One. Here man can find the solution to any problem, peace for the troubled mind, strength and power for the weary, health for the sick, and wisdom and light for the confused.

We will now partake of the wedding feast of Cana in our own mind. The marriage feast of Cana is a psychological drama taking place within your own mind. You, the reader, have all these psychological states within you.

(1) *And the third day there was a marriage in Cana of Galilee; and the mother of Jesus was there. Galilee* means your mind or consciousness; *Cana* means rod, stem, or your desire. The marriage is the mental and emotional union with your desire. The mother of Jesus, reminding him of lack, means your moods of lack, fear, and doubt which challenge your ideal or desire. Perhaps you are praying about something now while you read this. Is not there a challenge or opposition in your mind at the same time? This is the mother

---

* See my recent book *How to Attract Money*, second chapter concerning changing water into wine.

or feeling. Jesus means your own I AM-NESS or your consciousness.

(2) *And both Jesus was called, and his disciples, to the marriage.* The disciples are the faculties of your own mind which must be present at every marriage feast. You are attending a wedding of the mind with your desire, goal, or objective in life. You must call forth the bride or the correct feeling from the depths of yourself. Troward points out that "feeling is the law and the law is the feeling."

(3) *And when they wanted wine, the mother of Jesus saith unto him, They have no wine. Wine* in the Bible represents the objectification of your ideal. They have no wine is a reminder of lack, a suggestion of doubt. It refers to the tension, anxiety, and fear which grip the mind caused by the appearance of things, the verdict of the world, and the opinion of others. All these may challenge you.

How do you conquer these doubts and fears? The answer is given in the following: (4) *Woman, what have I to do with thee? mine hour is not yet come.* This is an oriental, graphic, and idiomatic expression signifying a complete mental rejection of all negative thoughts, and the recognition of the fact that there is but One Power, that the fear-thoughts have no power, and that there is nothing to sustain them. You figure out in your own mind that fear and doubt are a conglomeration of sinister shadows having no substance. You feast on the truth that the power lies in your own thought which causes the Spirit within to respond; now it is Omnipotence thinking and it has nothing to oppose it; therefore, you are assured of victory and triumph.

All negative thoughts and suggestions are recognized by you as illusions of power, for after all, there is only One Power—God—the Living Spirit Almighty within. This is the argumentative method used in prayer and practiced by Quimby one hundred years ago, which enables you to come to a conclusion or verdict in your own mind of the availability of the Omnipotence of God or Good at all times, in all emergencies, and in every crisis. As fear falls away, faith and confidence fill the mind; then you become united with your desire, and its fruition and blessings appear in your life.

(4) *Mine hour is not yet come; this means that a conviction is not yet reached in the mind.* (5) *His mother saith unto the servants, Whatsoever he saith unto you, do it.* The *servants* are our thoughts and feelings, in other words, our faculties and attitudes of mind. When you pray, you order your thoughts to give attention and devotion to what you wish to accomplish. You do not permit them to wander off. You do this in the same manner as you order employees in your store. You

want to be one with something highly desirable, such as health, true place, or right action; you can't afford to have your servants (thoughts) engaged in creating the opposite of what you seek. This would stultify your prayer-efforts and render all your action null and void. It would be praying two ways, and one would neutralize the other. You would thus be like the soldier marking time; i.e., you wouldn't get any place or arrive at any destination in your mind. *Your hour* has not come because you are not yet one with your goal. It has not been subjectively felt as true.

By illustration if you are praying for a healing of your eyes, and you notice they are not yet functioning perfectly, keep on praying maintaining your devotion and loyalty to the One Healing Presence now in action in your mind and body; you will win. The mother (feeling) in the first part of this prayer reminded you of lack. As you begin to meditate and pray, your mother (mood) changes to one of confidence, faith, and trust in the Only Power there is. The feeling of triumph and satisfaction is noted in the expression: *Whatsoever he saith unto you, do it* (6) *And there were set there six waterpots of stone, after the manner of the purifying of the Jews, containing two or three firkins apiece. The six waterpots of stone . . .* Dr. Nicoll says *water* is the psychological understanding of the truth (stone). He is referring to levels of spiritual knowledge or awareness. He refers to *stone* as taking truth literally; *water*, the psychological meaning behind the words, and *wine*, the inner joy which follows the inner transformation of man as he appropriates and applies the Truth of God.

Six refers to the six days of creation, or the creative fiat taking place in the consciousness of man. It represents a purifying, cleansing process which takes place or the change from the old to the new state. Six and sex are synonymous. The *six waterpots* refer to the psychological cycle that man goes through to bring about the subjective realization of his desire. This may endure for a moment, an hour, days, weeks, or months depending on the faith and state of consciousness of the student.

(7) *Jesus saith unto them, Fill the waterpots with water. And they filled them up to the brim.* In the prayer-process you become completely detached from the external world, and you meditate on the end or the solution until you reach the point where the inner certitude comes, whereby you know that you know. After the mental and emotional act is finished there is no desire to pray any more about it. Consequently, you know that it is finished. This is the meaning of *They filled them up to the brim.* You are actually filled full of the feeling of being what you long to be. When you fill your mind to the brim with the joy of answered

prayer, there is no room for negative, unresolved conflicts, such as ill will, resentment, or antagonism. Your entire mental attitude is absorbed in the reality of your desire.

(8) *And he saith unto them, Draw out now, and bear the governor of the feast. And they bare it.* The *governor of the feast* is the conscious mind which gets the idea or desire and places it in the subjective mind where it gestates and grows in the darkness; in due season it burst forth into manifestation. Whatever is impregnated in your subconscious mind is always objectified on the screen of space; then you are consciously aware of that which we formerly only felt subjectively as true.

(9) *When the ruler of the feast had tasted the water that was made wine, and knew not whence it was: (but the servants which drew the water knew;) the governor of the feast called the bridegroom.* The *ruler* of the feast is the conscious mind and its five senses. When the conscious mind becomes aware of *water made wine*, it becomes aware of the answered prayer. *Water* is also referred to as unconditioned consciousness, and *wine* is conditioned consciousness made manifest according to your belief. The *servants which drew the water* represent the mood of peace and confidence, and you know that your prayer is answered. *The governor of the feast called the bridegroom* means the thrill of the

joyful union with your good. You are now married to
your highest ideal.

(10) *And saith unto him, Every man at the begin-*
ning doth set forth good wine; and when men have well
drunk, then that which is worse: but thou hast kept the
good wine until now. This is true of every man when
he enters into truth. He sets out with high spirits and
ambitions. He is the new broom that sweeps clean and
he is full of good intentions. Oftentimes he forgets the
Source of his power and becomes drunk with power,
so to speak. In other words, he misuses the law and
selfishly takes advantage of his fellow man. We find
that many times men in high places become conceited,
opinionated, and arrogant. This is all due to ignorance of the law. The law is that power, security, and
riches are not to be obtained externally. They must
come from the treasure-house of consciousness. If you
remain in tune with the Infinite, you discover that you
are always drinking of the wine of life, love, joy, and
happiness. To the spiritually-minded man, God is the
Eternal Now and his good is present at every moment
of time and point of space.

Many people are drunk in the Biblical sense when
they are full of fear, grief, and other discordant states.
That is being drunk emotionally. The wonderful news
is that God *is* the Eternal Now. You can change you
thought this moment, and you change your destiny.

At any moment of the day you can gather your mental garments together and go on a great psychological feast of joy and happiness. Enter on the high watch by realizing the ever-availability of the God-Presence and its immediate response to your thought. All our good is in the Greater Now. We have to leave the present now (our limitation) and imagine the reality of our desire in the meditative state. What you have seen and felt in the Greater Now, your consciousness, you shall see objectified as you walk through time and space. We will see our beliefs expressed. Man is belief expressed. (Quimby).

(11) *This beginning of miracles did Jesus in Cana of Galilee, and manifested forth his glory; and his disciples believed on him.* (12) *After this he went down to Capernaum, he, and his mother, and his brethren, and his disciples: and they continued there not many days.* (13) *And the Jews' passover was at hand, and Jesus went up to Jerusalem,* (14) *And found in the temple those that sold oxen and sheep and doves, and the changers of money sitting:* (15) *And when he had made a scourge of small cords, he drove them all out of the temple, and the sheep, and the oxen; and poured out the changers' money, and overthrew the tables;* (16) *And said unto them that sold doves, Take these things hence; make not my Father's house an house of merchandise.* (17) *And his disciples*

remembered that it was written, The zeal of thine house hath eaten me up.

The *passover* represents a change of consciousness. Whenever man prays, he has celebrated the passover, because he passes psychologically from one mood to another. Your *feast of the passover* is to identify yourself with your ideal in your mind, remaining faithful to it until your prayer is answered.

Jesus going up to Jerusalem (city of peace) means turning in thought to the God-Presence within. When you assume the attitude of prayer, you are, in Biblical language, entering into the temple to pray; sometimes you find *money changers* there which represent the thieves and robbers who deprive you of your good.

In the prayer-process you must cast out error, fear, criticism, jealousy, resentment, and forgive everyone. Refuse positively and definitely to give power to external conditions or people. Throw out of your temple with the sword of truth, referred to in the Bible *as a scourge of small cords,* all fear, doubt, and worry. Claim that the God-Power is the only Power and that It is working on your behalf now. Chop the head off all other thoughts which pretend to have power. Ask these negative thoughts where they come from and what is their source? There is nothing to back them up and sustain them as there is no principle behind them.

Having come to a clear-cut decision in your mind where the Power is, you are charged with confidence, and your psychological journey is assured of success. Use this *scourge of small cords* regularly by making definite pronouncements of truth in your mind which cut into the negative state like whip cords and sever your connection with them completely.

(18) *Then answered the Jews and said unto him, What sign shewest thou unto us, seeing that thou doest these things?* Many people are always looking for proof—for a sign.

I heard a practitioner say one time that if God healed her hand, she would begin to teach again. This attitude is wrong. She is looking for a sign. I told her to go back to the platform and teach as if nothing had happened, knowing in her heart that God would honor her claim to a perfect hand functioning in Divine order. She followed the advice, and in a matter of months the partially paralyzed hand was functioning normally. The only sign is your inner feeling, your faith, or conviction. Your sign is the inner wave of peace and confidence which wells up within you. You wait for the answer to your prayer with the same assurance you would wait for the rising sun; this is the inner sign of faith.

(19) *Jesus answered and said unto them, Destroy this temple, and in three days I will raise it up.* The *three days*

refer to the trinity or the function of the mind—the first is desire; the second day is working with the desire until all fear is banished from consciousness; the third day refers to conviction or the feeling of being which I want to be.

(21) *But he spake of the temple of his body.* The body mentioned in verse twenty-one is the manifested world of man—the out-picturing of his consciousness.

(22) *When therefore he was risen from the dead, his disciples remembered that he had said this unto them; and they believed the scripture, and the word which Jesus had said. (23) Now when he was in Jerusalem at the passover, in the feast day, many believed in his name, when they saw the miracles which he did. (24) But Jesus did not commit himself unto them, because he knew all men. (25) And needed not that any should testify of man; for he knew what was in man.*

The essence of these verses is to remind man that we must never believe that a thing does not exist because we cannot see it. When we feel the thrill inside, we know that our prayer is answered and that it will come into manifestation.

Chapter 3

(1) *There was a man of the Pharisees, named Nicodemus, a ruler of the Jews: (2) The same came to Jesus by night, and said unto him, Rabbi, we know that thou art a teacher come from God: for no man can do these miracles that thou doest, except God be with him. (3) Jesus answered and said unto him, Verily, verily, I say unto thee, Except a man be born again, he cannot see the kingdom of God. (4) Nicodemus saith unto him, How can a man be born when he is old? can he enter the second time into his mother's womb, and be born? (5) Jesus answered, Verily, verily, I say unto thee, Except a man be born of water and of the Spirit, he cannot enter into the kingdom of God. (6) That which is born of the flesh is flesh; and that which is born of the Spirit is spirit. (7) Marvel not that I said unto thee, Ye must be born again. (8) The wind bloweth where it listeth, and thou hearest the sound thereof, but canst not tell whence it cometh, and whither it goeth: so is every one that is born of the Spirit. (9) Nicodemus answered and said unto him,*

How can these things be? (10) Jesus answered and said unto him, Art thou a master of Israel, and knowest not these things? (11) Verily, verily, I say unto thee, We speak that we do know, and testify that we have seen; and ye receive not our witness. (12) If I have told you earthly things, and ye believe not, how shall ye believe, if I tell you of heavenly things? (13) And no man hath ascended up to heaven, but he that came down from heaven, even the Son of man which is in heaven. (14) And as Moses lifted up the serpent in the wilderness, even so must the Son of man be lifted up; (15) That whosoever believeth in him should not perish, but have eternal life. (16) For God so loved the world, that he gave his only begotten Son, that whosoever believeth in him should not perish, but have everlasting life. (17) For God sent not his Son into the world to condemn the world; but that the world through him might be saved.

Before giving the wonderful inner meaning of this story, I am going to show the marvelous teaching method outlined in this chapter of the Bible. It has often been remarked that the worst teaching takes place in the units of higher education—the high school or college—while the best teaching methods are found to be used in the kindergarten where children really grow up to successive levels of emergent consciousness. In the former, the teacher usually lectures to the pupils making no effort to probe the listeners for tangible signs of understanding and the ability to apply the principle and techniques present.

The riveting of new *ideas* and new concepts is to be accomplished only by the patient preparation of the learner's consciousness by skilled presentation, questioning, skilled recapitulation, reviewing, and summarization of the field of content; then should follow the important pedagogical step—application and use of the principles taught. This last step will correspond to the Master's injunction, Go *and do likewise.* Let us look at the following method of teaching.

(a) The scene of Jesus and Nicodemus comments: The environment is the night scene protecting a distinguished but timid and fearful pupil; the subject of instruction is "the birth from above"; the aim of the teacher was probably to bring about a mystic change in the life of the pupil. The method used was conversation including questions, answers, a remarkable, concrete illustration of the working of the spirit (JOHN 3:8), and the exhilaration of surprise (JOHN 3:10). Another striking method of the Bible method of teaching is given in the case of Jesus and the woman of Samaria (JOHN 4:1 to 42). A complete teaching situation is indicated in the unfoldment of this lesson with the factors—master, pupil, environment, subject matter, aim, and method.

(b) Find the following pedagogical techniques in the situation: the point of contact between pupil and teacher, and the use of attention and interest through surprise power, the method of teaching utilized the principle of personal association. The use of the pupils' apperceptive background encouraged the comment. "In that saidst thou truly"—living water and thirst—and various problems raised during the conversation, such as the woman's problems used as a point of contact causing an awakening of conscience and leading to the theological problem, felt and stated by the pupil, "Where shall God be worshiped?"

The pedagogical interplay illustrated in these lessons indicate the essential difficulty of the job of teaching the mystic content of metaphysics in such a way that the hidden springs of consciousness are touched, come alive, and produce real seekers of Him (God-consciousness) Whom to know aright is Life Eternal (complete identification with the Self—the

Father within). The teacher of the hidden meaning of the Bible has the joy of leading the pupil to see, hear, taste, touch, and smell at higher levels of consciousness for *in the Father's house there are many mansions.*

The explanation of the story is as follows: *Nicodemus* means man groping toward the Light, the presence of which he has become dimly aware. He is aware only of the physical birth which is typical of the man whose senses are glued to material things. You could look upon this as a dialogue taking place between your intellect and the Deeper Self within. Nicodemus is judging from outer appearance and evidence, "for no man can do these miracles that thou doest except God be with him." He is still wedded to the old thought, yet is dissatisfied and is seeking Light. Being a *man of the Pharisees* means that he is one who adheres to the letter of the law, but lacks the spirit which giveth life. He is the worldly-minded man who fails to realize that his own consciousness is God, the Creative Power within himself, his Redeemer and Saviour. He has no internal vision or perception of truth as yet.

In verse two *coming to Jesus* means coming to the truth or light. The answer given him by Jesus which symbolizes truth is that *except he be born again he cannot see the kingdom of God.* Nicodemus (five-sense-man) does not understand the working of the mind or spirit within represented in the statement, *the same came to Jesus by night*; this is a symbol of spiritual darkness, yearning for Wisdom.

To be born again means to think in a new way, to undergo an internal transformation of the mind by realizing and knowing that God is the Spiritual Power within which can be contacted through man's thought, thereby bringing about the rebirth of consciousness. Nicodemus judged by the visible state. When we are born again, we judge by the invisible state. Everything in the Bible is intended to convey a special meaning, and the main point is to know what is meant. We are not at all concerned whether such a conversation actually took place between two men two thousand years ago or not. We are primarily interested in what it means to us, and how we can use the drama to rise in the knowledge of God. The psychological life-germ is the meat we seek. As you read this story you are reading about yourself and probably asking the same question as Nicodemus.

In teaching you may cite a hypothetical case and various incidents in order to illustrate your point. The illumined men who wrote the Bible undoubtedly invented many of the characters in their very vivid imagination in the same way as some of our screen writers invent certain characters.

Shakespeare delved into some of the ancient legends and myths and meditating on their meaning brought forth, through his artistic and awakened mind, allegories of vital interest to all of us. He mentally clothed them in the garments of men and women and breathed into them the breath of life. All the characters he portrays live in all of us.

Likewise, the characters portrayed in the Bible and their experiences are true in the sense that they are applicable to all of us and truer than if they were actual historic events occurring on a certain date, in a certain country, and confined to a certain man or woman.

The *rebirth* spoken of here is a new level of consciousness. Many think of rebirth as coming back again to this plane. Probably that was also in the mind of Nicodemus. Others think that *to be born again* is to join some church and accept some personal saviour. "How can a man be born when he is old?" The average man thinks of God as far off. He considers heaven as a plane to which he goes when he leaves this plane. He fails to see that anyone can enter the second time into the mother's womb, psychologically, and be reborn spiritually. Man can enter the Womb of God (his own consciousness) again and again and be reborn to higher levels. There is no end. *Your womb* is your inner feeling—your subjective nature.

Here is how *you* may enter the womb of God and be reborn: Get still and quiet by relaxing the mind and body. Detach yourself from the old way of thinking and form a new concept or estimate of yourself. Imagine and feel the reality of the new ideal; live with it; envelop it in love; woo it; then the ideal will be resurrected in you, and you will become a changed man.*

I knew a murderer one time who confessed to me that he had killed a man. He had an intense desire to transform himself and be reborn mentally and spiritually. I wrote down the qualities and attributes of God for him. He began to still the wheels of his mind. For fifteen or twenty minutes several times daily he would quietly, silently, and lovingly claim and feel that God's love, peace, beauty, glory, and light were flowing through his mind and heart, purifying, cleansing, healing, and restoring his soul. As he did this regularly, these qualities came out of his mother's womb, which was his own feeling or mood as he prayed. One night this man's whole mind and body, as well as the room he was in, became a blaze of light. He was actually blinded like Paul by the light for a while. He said to me that all he could remember was that he knew the whole world was within him and that he felt the ecstasy and rapture of God's love. His feeling was indescribable. It was in other words the moment which lasts forever. He was a changed man. Truly he

---

* See my book *The Meaning of Reincarnation* pages 22–23.

expressed the real incarnation of God in his mind and heart. He began to teach others how to live. He was born of water and the spirit. Water will take the shape of any vessel into which it is poured, so will your mental attitudes and beliefs assume form and shape in your world.

Spirit is a feeling, a mood, or animated state of consciousness. *To be born of water and the spirit* is, therefore, to begin to contemplate God and His Love in a new way; to get a new mental perspective, and to begin to feel the joy of the answered prayer within you. When we see the word *verily* in the Bible, it points the finger at a statement of truth which instructs us to stop, look, and listen. *To be born again* means spiritual rebirth—the birth of God in man. *Be not conformed to the world: but be ye transformed by the renewing of your mind.* ROMANS 12:2. Cease being a grubworm and become the butterfly. Experience the inner transformation; rise with wings of faith and understanding, and soar aloft over present difficulties and limitations. The wings within you are unused. Don't wait for God to do something. God will do nothing for you except through your own thought. God has given you everything. You are here to awaken through your mind, feeling, and consciousness. The transformation you are seeking you give to yourself psychologically and emotionally. The phrase *born of the flesh* means the mind saturated with world beliefs and opinions. You are born of the flesh if you let the world-mind and the race-belief govern you. Turn within and let your mind be governed by God's ideas. You will then be *born of the spirit.*

In verse eight, the *wind* is the spirit and takes form according to our belief or conviction. The *sound thereof* means our feeling, subjective embodiment, or conviction. In other words we hear the sound of our belief. We can never tell how, when, where, or through what source our prayers will be answered; this is the secret of the Father within. *His ways are past finding out. Rest in the silence,* and the moment you think not the *son of man* will appear with healing on his wings (objectification of your desire). As every man is born of the spirit, so is his every manifestation born.

When you say, "Why is my prayer not answered?" the question answers itself. In asking that question we indicate doubt and fear. Have faith, trust God like you trusted your mother when in her arms, you saw love there. When doubt enters, focus on your ideal, and through frequent occupancy of the mind, you will find your faith grows.

These truths are so simple and direct that we walk over them, failing to see clearly what is meant, and we exclaim like Nicodemus, "How can these things be?" Heretofore we thought it was necessary to have wealth, power, influence, etc. in order to get what we wanted. The reverse of this is true. We simply claim what we want in consciousness and know that it is so; then it will come to pass according to our mental attitude. *According to your faith be it unto you.* MATTHEW 9:29.

I will now touch on the important verses of the rest of the chapter. (14) *As Moses lifted up the serpent in the wilderness, even so must the Son of man be lifted up.* The *serpent* is a symbol of the Healing Presence within man; the *Son of man* is the idea, desire, concept, or ambition you wish to manifest; *man* in the Bible means mind. You must play the *role* of Moses which means a triumphant attitude of mind believing in One Spiritual Power (I AM). As you lift your concept up in mind to the point of acceptance, you will experience the healing, or the answer to your prayer. You are lifting the serpent up when you contemplate the true nature of God.

(16) *For God so loved the world, that he gave his only begotten Son, that whosoever believeth in him should not perish, but have everlasting life.*

If you are sick, God has given you the only begotten Son—a mind. You must learn how to use it. You will find that when you use your mind in the right way, you can have health, wealth, and peace of mind. Your desire is your savior; by identifying yourself with your desire you will mentally embody and manifest it. The world is your outer expression. God's Love for you is that He has given you Himself. You have all the equipment necessary to overcome all difficulties and obstacles. Believe in this Power, and you shall not perish through pain, misery, and suffering, but you shall lead the abundant life spoken of by Jesus.

(27) *A man can receive nothing, except it be given him from heaven.* This means consciousness is the cause of all. In other words all your experiences are out-picturings of inner mental states—the heavens of your own mind.

(30) *He must increase, but I must decrease.* This means intuition or the Wisdom of God must increase and grow, and the intellectual, materialistic concept of life must diminish. Our intellect must be anointed with the Wisdom of God; then we will use our conscious, reasoning mind to carry out the dictates of the Divine.

(34) *For he whom God hath sent speaketh the words of God: for God giveth not the spirit by measure unto him.* We speak the word of God when we feel the truth of what we affirm; this is the Holy Spirit, feeling of wholeness, or oneness; then there is no doubt.

Chapter 4

(1) When therefore the Lord knew how the Pharisees had heard that Jesus made and baptised more disciples than John, (2) (Through Jesus himself baptised not, but his disciples,) (3) He left Judaea, and departed again into Galilee. (4) And he must needs go through Samaria. (5) Then cometh he to a city of Samaria, which is called Sychar, near to the parcel of ground that Jacob gave to his son Joseph.

Jesus' entrance into Galilee (conscious mind) sets forth the increased awareness of God's Presence welling up from the subjective depths (Judaea). Here is a marvelous lesson in prayer, teaching all of us how to eradicate racial, political, and religious prejudice. *Sychar* means idolatry or the worship of false gods, i.e., giving our attention to anything negative. In prayer we must separate our thoughts and give our attention to God and His Omnipotence and give power to nothing else. To give power to conditions, circumstances, and external causes is to practice idolatry. *Joseph* means disciplined imagination or our capacity to imagine the end and feel its reality.

(6) *Now Jacob's well was there. Jesus therefore, being wearied with his journey, sat thus on the well: and it was about the sixth hour.*

Jacob's well refers to the inside of man, his soul or subjective, and emotional life. In this well lay all wisdom, knowledge, and power. It is the infinite storehouse of all forms of immaterial life. From this soul or subjective self are born all the experiences of man. We must drink from the great unconscious depth within us.

(7) *There cometh a woman of Samaria to draw water: Jesus saith unto her, Give me to drink.* (8) (*For his disciples were gone away unto the city to buy meat.*)

The woman of Samaria is the feeling of lack and limitation. It represents a prejudiced mind full of sectarian beliefs, etc. Jesus, our desire, says to us, "*Give me to drink*"; that is really the Higher Self or God-Self speaking through us telling us to move out of our limitation or problem. Whenever we have a problem or difficulty, the answer is always knocking at the door in the form of a desire. We must drink of inspiration, guidance, strength, and power. *His disciples* are our thoughts, feelings, and general attitudes which assume the attitude of prayer in the city of our mind where they *buy meat* or become strengthened through faith in the Omnipotent Power on which they are focused.

(9) *Then saith the woman of Samaria unto him, How is it that thou, being a Jew, askest drink of me, which am a woman of Samaria? for the Jews have no dealings with the Samaritans.* This verse indicates confusion, racial prejudice, and a disturbed mind.

(10) *Jesus answered and said unto her, If thou knewest the gift of God, and who it is that saith to thee, Give me to drink; thou wouldest have asked of him, and he would have given thee living water.*

The gift of God is our desire. If man knew that his Awareness was God, and that his desire was simply life urging him forward, he would turn within to the Source and claim his desire as a reality now. *The woman of Samaria* represents that type of mind which believes in an external God and does not know that the God-Presence is submerged in the Great Unconscious within and is governed by five-sense evidence which dominates her. A psychological change and a spiritual awakening process is denoted in the following verse, (11) *The woman saith unto him, Sir, thou hast nothing to draw with, and the well is deep: from whence then hast thou that living water?*

The woman in us, means our doubts and fears are based on false beliefs about God and His laws. *Thou hast nothing to draw with* refers to the fact that man thinks in order to get what he wants, he must have a prop. He must have a bucket to draw with. He takes things literally and imagines that it is necessary to belong to some church or sect in order to be saved. As long as a man does not know that the Kingdom of God is within, he will postulate it as outside; furthermore, he believes the external world is causative from which come all his confusion, hates, prejudices, and doubts. He is always asking *from whence hast thou that living water? Living water* means inspiration, truth, healing, guidance, or whatever man needs for spiritual refreshment. The old beliefs are that we need ritual, ceremonies, altars, and churches in which we may worship, pray, and petition. The old race beliefs, traditions, creed, and dogma raise their heads and challenge us. The old thoughts that we are the playthings of chance, that there are entities and powers outside ourselves which we must oppose and fight—all these die and disappear so that we might experience the living water—the Kingdom of Heaven within. *Truth* is the sword causing us to sever and give up all our false concepts, beliefs in personalities and tradition. Sometimes there is a poignant parting with these old ideas. Instead of giving power to historical characters, we must have reliance and confidence in our own subjective depths which is the creative medium responding always according to the level of our belief.

(12) *Art thou greater than our father Jacob, which gave us the well, and drank thereof himself, and his children, and his cattle?*

The challenge continues. In other words, this is the *well* of traditional belief, or the old concept of an anthropomorphic god to whom we beg and make our supplications. This is usually a god of wrath created out of the figment of man's imagination, an inscrutable and tyrannical being. Men challenge the truth that God is their own indwelling, formless awareness. "Closer is He than breathing, nearer than hands and feet!" They point to their church and its dogma with a long record of saints, martyrs, prophets, and its ritual, ceremonies, pomp, and power. They say our fathers worshiped and died for all this. Men die as readily for superstition as they do for truth. They refuse to accept the truths of their own psychological capacity to be independent and free from limitation, troubles, pain, and misery of all kinds. Millions are governed, controlled, and dominated by the ideas, erroneous opinions, and false beliefs of men long since dead. They are living in the dead past described in the Bible as *living among tombs*. The *tomb* represents the records of the dead past. When man refuses to test his opinions and seek the right answer, he remains in bondage to these dead dogmas and man-made traditions.

Man can find the ideas and forms of truth that will lead him to a higher state of himself. He can discover a science of life, knowledge, and a wisdom enabling him to attain health, happiness, and peace of mind; but first he must divest himself of the false knowledge and beliefs which rob him of his true state.

In order to become a chemist, it is necessary to study the laws of chemistry, chemical equation, reactions, etc. To get the wrong idea or false knowledge of the subject would be highly dangerous. Imagine studying under a teacher who does not understand chemistry himself; this would be a case of the blind leading the blind. Ask yourself where your religion came from. Trace the history. Investigate and explore these beliefs. Track them back to their hiding places which rest in man-made tyranny and lust for power. *In vain they do worship me, teaching for doctrines the commandments of men.* (MATTHEW 15:9).

(13) *Jesus answered and said unto her, Whosoever drinketh of this water shall thirst again:* (14) *But whosoever drinketh of the water that I shall give him shall never thirst; but the water that I shall give him shall be in him a well of water springing up into everlasting life.*

Many do not know where the waters of life exist. When you speak of water, man begins to think in terms of drinking water and fails to see that you are speaking of the refreshing power of spiritual values. Man seeks without for security, integrity, peace, and happiness; yet, all the while, these powers come from within.

I told our class on Ouspensky's inner teachings about a man who offered a million dollars to his physician if he would heal his boy. The good doctor explained that medical science had done all that was possible and the only thing that could save his boy was prayer. The man said, "I don't know how to pray." You see how thirsty he was? He did not know where to drink from, or that the fountain of life was within him. He did not know how to drink of faith, confidence, and trust in an Infinite Healing Presence. The doctor taught him how to pray and his son lived.

You cannot buy peace of mind, health, joy, or faith in God. You cannot purchase Wisdom. All the real gifts of life are intangible; they come from the Spirit. They are the Eternal Verities.

Let us see a different level of meaning in all the stories of the Bible. All of us can reach a higher potential within ourselves; by correct knowledge and scientific mental practice we can attain a higher level. Enthrone now the ideas of peace, security, and happiness in your mind. Live with these ideas until they become subjective embodiments; then you will never thirst again. *The well of water springing up into everlasting life* is the Living Spirit Almighty within; by meditation and prayer we can enjoy the fruits of the spirit down through the corridors of time until time shall be no more.

(15) *The woman saith unto him, Sir, give me this water, that I thirst not, neither come hither to draw.* (16) *Jesus saith unto her, Go, call thy husband, and come hither.*

Our *husband* should be God or Good. We should see to it that our mind or consciousness is impregnated only with noble, lovely, and wise concepts. This is what happens, however, in the majority of cases: Our five senses become impregnated with all kinds of false knowledge, sundry concepts, and errors of all kinds are constantly impinging on the receptive media of the mind. The avalanche of sights, sounds, false beliefs, and fears are conveyed through our five senses which impregnate our mind, becoming five false husbands whereas Wisdom should be our husband at all times. The result is that the emotional nature of man is constantly reproducing in his experiences the limitations impressed on his emotional nature by the unillumined five senses.

The Bible says, *Thy maker is thine husband. The husband shall be head of the wife,* which means the idea you entertain impregnates your emotional or subjective nature. When our thoughts are God's thoughts, we are *calling the husband*.

(17) *The woman answered and said, I have no husband. Jesus said unto her, Thou hast well said, I have no husband: (18) For thou hast had five husbands; and he whom thou now hast is not thy husband: in that saidst thou truly.*

The person in a confused state of lack and limitation does not have God or Good as a husband; hence, the answer, *I have no husband*. When we dwell in the mental atmosphere of fear and anxiety, we are not married to God; therefore, we do not have a true husband (a disciplined, spiritualized, conscious mind). Is your religious belief satisfying you? Does it give you comfort, peace of mind, and inner growth? Ask yourself, are all my ideas based on the truth of God?

(19) *The woman saith unto him, Sir, I perceive that thou art a prophet. (20) Our fathers worshipped in this mountain; and ye say, that in Jerusalem is the place where man ought to worship. (21) Jesus saith unto her, Woman, believe me, the hour cometh, when ye shall neither in this mountain, nor yet in Jerusalem, worship the Father. (22) Ye worship ye know not what: we know what we worship: for salvation is of the Jews. (23) But the hour cometh, and now is, when the true worshippers shall worship the Father in spirit and in truth: for the Father seeketh such to worship him. (24) God is a Spirit:*

*and they that worship him must worship him in spirit
and in truth.*

Many people think that the only place to worship
is in a church made of brick and stone or at a certain
shrine. Here we are told that we should worship God
in spirit and in truth. To *worship* means to give your
attention to, to be worthy, to be devoted. A *church* is
a symbol of a mental and emotional state dedicated
to wisdom, love, and truth. Your church is the inner
sanctuary of your soul. The *choir* represents the inner
feeling of joy, the exalted mood, which follows the
silent contemplation of God. The church is within
(assemblage of Divine ideas, attitudes, and faculties
focused on God). The *high priest* is within (feeling).
God is within (our consciousness or I AM-NESS).

Salvation is of the Jews. This does not refer to any
race of people. One of the meanings of the word *Jew*
refers to the intellect illumined by the Light. Salvation, or the solution, comes to the man whose intellect is anointed by the Wisdom of God. The true Jew
knows the Messiah is within; his faith in God is his
savior. He trusts in the Infinite Intelligence to respond
to his prayer. He knows the Messiah that is to come is
the solution, or answer, to his prayer.

Let these truths which we have elaborated on here
become alive in you, forming a living spring of fresh
and wonderful meanings; then you will hunger no

more, neither will you thirst any more. You will drink from the fountain of living waters; God shall wipe away all tears from your eyes, and there shall be no more crying.

We will now touch on the main highlights of the rest of the chapter. In other words, we will discuss the *meat* of it.

(29) *Come, see a man, which told me all things that ever I did: is not this the Christ?*

Christ is your awakening to the truth or illumined reason. You are now aware that all things that ever happened to you have been due to the limitations imposed upon you by your five senses; furthermore, as you look back upon your life, you realize you have constantly given witness to these false impregnations. The whole conversation or agreement between Jesus and the woman at the well is the argument that takes place in the average person's mind between the appearance of things, i.e., what his five senses say and what he desires to be. There is a challenge in his mind. The Greater Self within you says, "If you would only believe you are now what you long to be, you would become it." The lesser you says, "It's too good to be true. Look at the evidence. The well is deep, and I have nothing to draw with." Suspend the evidence of your senses. Go within, shut the door, and begin to feel you are what you long to be. Continue to do so until you qualify your consciousness; then a sense of rest and peace will come. You will objectify what you subjectively accepted.

(35) *Say not ye, There are yet four months, and then cometh harvest? behold, I say unto you, Lift up your eyes, and look on the fields; for they are white already to harvest.*

The *meat we eat is the will of God. The will* of God for all men is the abundant life which is the mental appropriation of all things good. We must not say that it is *four months to the harvest.* In other words we must cease postponing our good. Your good, your desire, exists now in the next dimension or higher level of being. Peace, health, harmony, wisdom, etc. are all within you. Don't postpone peace; accept it now!

For instance the home you wish to sell: Realize it is already sold in Divine Mind. Accept that mentally; then the Infinite Intelligence will bring you and the buyer together. The invisible idea is the reality behind everything. That is why it is not four months to the harvest. All states of consciousness exists in the Greater Now within you, so does all Wisdom and Knowledge.

Frequently you hear, "He told me all that I ever did." The past is an open book to a psychic, intuitive person. In a partially subjective state many people can tune in with the subconscious mind of the other and read the past easily; for anything that has ever happened in a man's life is impressed and registered in the inner, subliminal consciousness.

(44) *For Jesus himself testified, that a prophet hath no honour in his own country.*

The *country* in Bible language refers to a state of consciousness. We must leave our present state of mind and move psychologically to another realm of mind where we meditate on spiritual processes and functions. When we still the mind and engage our attention on our good, the Power of God flows through the focal-point of attention. We have now moved into another country, because we have reached a new state of consciousness or concept of ourselves.

(50) *Go thy way; thy son liveth.* (52) *Yesterday at the seventh hour the fever left him.*

The above quotations are really the essence of the balance of the chapter. Here we are given a lesson in absent treatment. Actually there is no absence in the One Presence when treating or praying for the healing of another; it is necessary to discipline and cleanse your mind of the fears and opinions of mankind; you must do this emphatically and decisively. The next step is to turn to the Healing Presence within and feel that the patient is free from his false beliefs and opinions, knowing at the same time that your thoughts of health, peace, and happiness are God in action. Your inner knowing that harmony, health, and peace are the true gifts of God for your patient is also resurrected in your patient's mind.

He sent his word and healed them. When another is ill, he calls for help and alleviation. You can take his request accepting his healing in your mind to the point of conviction. When you reach the point of complete, mental acceptance, that is called the seventh hour, the Sabbath, or stillness of the mind, knowing that your prayer is answered. This is the meaning of the Bible statement *at the seventh hour his fever left him.*

Chapter 5

(1) After this there was a feast of the Jews; and Jesus went up to Jerusalem. (2) Now there is at Jerusalem by the sheep market a pool, which is called in the Hebrew tongue Bethesda, having five porches. (3) In these lay a great multitude of impotent folk, of blind, halt, withered, waiting for the moving of the water. (4) For an angel went down at a certain season into the pool, and troubled the waters whosoever then first after the troubling of the water stepped in was made whole of whatsoever disease he had. (5) And a certain man was there, which had an infirmity thirty and eight years. (6) When Jesus saw him lie, and knew that he had been now a long time in that case, he saith unto him, Wilt thou be made whole? (7) The impotent man answered him, Sir, I have no man, when the water is troubled, to put me into the pool: but while I am coming, another steppeth down before me. (8) Jesus saith unto him, Rise, take up thy bed and walk.

A *feast* represents a psychological feast in which we meditate on that which we want. *Jerusalem* means at peace, or the consciousness of peace. *Jesus going to Jerusalem* means stilling the mind and contemplating peace. *Bethesda* is a haven of rest. You enter the rest when you detach your consciousness from the world and think of God and His Laws. Still the wheels of your mind and think of the Living Spirit Almighty within you. At that moment you are in the *pool of Bethesda*.

The five porches means our five senses. Our sense-evidence denies what we pray for; furthermore, we have been impregnated with all kinds of limitations and false beliefs through the five senses. Our hopes, dreams, aspirations, and ideals which we have failed to realize represent the multitude of impotent folk, blind, halt, and withered within us.

The sheep market means that prayer is like a market place where we exchange one thing for another. *Sheep* represent the lovely states we wish to embody, consequently we must buy or exchange the mood of lack for the mood of opulence, the feeling of sickness for the feeling and picture of perfect health. You could call the conscious mind the market-place wherein we may buy, sell, or exchange our ideas, concepts, desires, false beliefs, doubts, etc. The average five-sense man who judges by appearance and is involved in external phenomena only seems to be waiting for something to happen, not knowing that the Creative Power is within enabling him to give life to his ideas and desires of his heart.

We are told an angel disturbs the pool. The word *angel* comes from angelus, meaning an attitude of mind, new idea, or desire which wells up in your heart. Your desire disturbs the pool which is your mind. You will have no real peace until your desire is realized.

As you read this book, maybe your desire is to sing on television but you find yourself blocked. Perhaps you are plagued with doubt, anxiety, fear, or you permitted the negative suggestions of others to depress you. You are told *whosoever stepped in first was made whole.* You must realize once and for all that no one can really get into the pool (Presence of God) before you, for the simple reason that your own thought is the only power. The suggestions of others, the race mind, and its beliefs have no power over you. External conditions and suggestions of others are not causative. You would have to permit yourself to move in thought negatively first.

You are *first in the pool* when you know God is One and Indivisible; this Presence is Unity. There are no divisions or quarrels in it; moreover there is nothing to challenge Omnipotence. When you think of God and His Healing Power, you are one with the Almighty, with Omnipotence Itself; then it is actually God thinking and your thought or prayer will and must come to pass. All fear and negative thoughts of the world cannot now enter into your mind, because you are focused on God, the Omnipotent One. How could anyone, therefore, deprive you of your good? That is why it is written, "One with God is a majority." The Source is Love; It knows no fear. Troward says, "There cannot be two Infinites as one would cancel out the other."

You are always hearing some people say, "It was John's fault." "Only for Mary or Susan I would have been promoted." They are always blaming others for their troubles and misfortunes. In Biblical language they are saying, "While I am coming, another steppeth down before me."

When you pray for a healing, do you permit the stars to step in your way? Do you give them preference by saying that due to the configuration of the planets, you can't be healed now? If you are, you are double-minded and not recognizing the Supremacy of the One Power. Your allegiance is divided, and nothing happens. You have a conflict in the mind. Come to an inner stop and believe in the God that made the stars. Why worship a confluence of atoms and molecules in the heavens.

This is how you get into the pool of the Holy Omnipresence which forever burns its Lamp of Love in your heart and keeps its Light of Life forever on your path. No one can say, "I AM," for you. It is first person, present tense. If you speak to your sister you say, "You are" When speaking in third person, you say, "He is or they are".

One of our students in the Bible class on the *Book of John* said to herself, "I possess the power to say 'I AM'. No one can say it for me. I now believe I am what I wish to be. I live, move, and have my being in that mental atmosphere and no person, place, or thing can get in before me or prevent me from being what I long to be; for, according to my belief, is it done unto me." She had a remarkable demonstration using the above prayer.

Cease giving power to external circumstances, the weather, other people, and the world of effect. Cease making an effect a cause. There is only One Power, the Spirit within you, your own awareness or consciousness. If you wish to be first in the pool, you will stop transferring the Power within you to others and the worship of strange gods and ideas. Accept your wholeness, completeness, and perfection now. The *angel who disturbed your pool,* or consciousness, is your desire for health. The *impotent man* is the man who does not know where the Power is. He believes it is outside himself. As he gradually awakens to the truth of his own being, he realizes that the Healing Presence is within and that he can contact it.

The *thirty and eight years* in the numerical symbology or science of the Bible means the conviction of God's Presence and coming of age spiritually. The number *thirty* refers to the Trinity or the creative working of our own mind; the *eight* means octave or man's capacity to rise higher through knowledge of mental and spiritual laws.

The Trinity for healing is:

1st.   Recognition of Spiritual Power as Supreme and Omnipotent.
2nd.   Your desire for health.
3rd.   Claiming, feeling, and believing in your perfect health, knowing the Almighty Power responds according to your faith and mental acceptance of the idea of perfect health.

The number *eight* is added when healing takes place. Eight is composed of two circles representing the synchronous or harmonious interaction of your conscious and subconscious mind, or idea and feeling. When your desire and your emotional nature agree, there is no longer any quarrel between the two, and a healing follows. All those reading this wonderful chapter of the Bible may now apply it and work wonders in their own life.

The command by Jesus, or your own illumined reason, "Rise, take up thy bed and walk" is your own inner conviction which speaks to you, telling you that you are healed. It is the command on the inside. You have taken up your bed (truth) and walked the earth a free man. All this happens on the sabbath.

The sabbath is the inner certitude or sense of stillness which follows true prayer. It is that point of consciousness where you are unconcerned, unmoved, and undisturbed, because you know that, just as surely as the sun rises in the morning, so will there be a resurrection of your desire. When you believe in your heart, you can't say, "How?" When?" "Where?" or "Through what source?" When you have reached the end of your mental journey, psychologically speaking, you don't say, "How?"

By example, when you arrive at Chicago, you don't say, "How did I get here?" You are there. As you walk in the ever-availability of the God-Presence and live in that Spiritual Atmosphere, you are always in the sabbath.

(9) *And immediately the man was made whole, and took up his bed, and walked: and on the same day was the sabbath.*

Millions celebrate the sabbath on the outside, thinking it is a sin to drive a nail in a piece of wood, etc., all of which is absurd. They do not know that the sabbath is on the inside. They fail to realize that it is celebrated every day when man abides in the consciousness of the ever-availability of goodness, truth, beauty, and abundance during the whole course of his life.

We will cover the essential highlights of the rest of the chapter by explaining the key verses and avoiding as much repetition as possible. Many of the verses overlap and have already been covered and explained previously.

(17) *My Father worketh hitherto, and I work.*

It is necessary to have cooperation and agreement between the two levels of mind for the harmonious expression of our ideals. There must be no argument or quarrel in our emotional or intellectual side; both must agree. When the two synchronize and agree on anything, it is established and made manifest. If you think about awakening at 5:00 A.M. prior to sleep, the deeper level of your mind will awaken you. This is a very simple illustration of the meaning of the above passage.

(22) *For the Father judgeth no man, but hath committed all judgment unto the Son.*

The *Son* means idea, thought, mind, or expression. It is our own mind which judges and condemns. *As a man thinketh in his heart, so is he.* We pass judgment on ourselves by our thought, or concept of ourselves.

(30) *As I hear, I judge . . .*

What do we hear? Do we hear good news about ourselves and others, or do we entertain negative attitudes?

(23) *That all men should honour the Son, even as they honour the Father . . .*

We should honour the Son—meaning we should have a loftier concept of ourselves. We should thrill to this concept, envelop it in love, after which we embody it. If we are not radiant, happy, exalted, and joyous, we are not honoring the Father.

(30) *I can of mine own self do nothing: as I hear, I judge: and my judgment is just.*

This verse means that the conscious, reasoning mind of man is not creative. It is the subjective self of man that has the answer, sees all, and knows all. Our *judgment is just* in the sense that action and reaction are equal. Man sets the law of mind in action based on his judgment. All mental action, such as decisions arrived at, things reasoned out, take place in the conscious mind. The absolute does not reason. Judgment, the conclusion arrived at in your mind, invokes the automatic response of the law in accordance with the decision or thought.

If your judgment or decision is wise, you will experience the just response of your judgment. If man errs in his judgment and makes a serious mistake, he will experience the response or just reaction which some people call vengeance. There is no imbalance, no favoritism in the law. Action and reaction are always equal and all of us know, or should know, this from our own experience.

(39) *Search the scriptures; for in them ye think ye have eternal life: and they are they which testify of me.*

Men search the scriptures and quote them freely. They have the letter of the law, but lack the spirit of the law which giveth life. The worship of God must be an inner awareness and not just ritual, ceremonies, forms, and liturgy or biblical quotes. There must be an inner mystical elevation, a sincere desire to be one with the Father in spirit and in love; then revelation will be certain to follow.

(46) *For had ye believed Moses, ye would have believed me: for he wrote of me.*

Moses means to draw out of the deep our desire, goal, or ideal. If we believed in the reality of the desire or ideal, knowing it already exists in another dimension of mind, we would believe in God or our good; for our desire, when realized, would save us from any predicament. It would be our savior.

Chapter 6

(1) After these things Jesus went over the sea of Galilee, which is the sea of Tiberias. (2) And a great multitude followed him, because they saw his miracles which he did on them that were diseased. (3) And Jesus went up into a mountain, and there he sat with his disciples. (4) And the passover, a feast of the Jews, was nigh. (5) When Jesus then lifted up his eyes, and saw a great company come unto him, he saith unto Philip, Whence shall we buy bread, that these may eat? (6) And this he said to prove him: for he himself knew what he would do.

This parable deals with inner transformation. *The feeding of the five thousand people* represents the hungry, confused, depressed, and fearful thoughts which follow us psychologically all day long. The *great multitude* is composed of the messages coming from the external five senses. We have to feed the blind, the halt, the hungry, and lame thoughts in ourselves. We must give spiritual food and knowledge to such blind people (thoughts).

For example, men have thoughts in their minds which speak to them and tell them that heaven is up in the sky some place, and hell is something below them. When men learn that they make their own heaven (harmony, peace, and joy) and hell (pain, misery, and suffering) by wrong thinking or failure to think, the blind thoughts begin to see and understand the cause of their trouble. It might then be said that the blind see.

This above story in the Bible is intended to teach man to establish a center of power within him independent of external things. The average man believes only in the reality that his senses show him. He seems to think that the external world with all its events is the cause of everything. Man is spiritually blind when he does not know that he has the innate capacity and ability to bring his ideals to fruition regardless of external conditions or sense evidence. The Self of man moves through all restrictions and knows no opposition; it is Omnipotent.

I gave a lecture in New Zealand in 1955 during a world lecture tour dealing with this parable. A man in the audience at one of the lectures said he couldn't see how his son could be healed. He was spiritually blind; he fed that blind state by claiming the Infinite Healing

Power was transforming his son. He was previously deaf to the truth; now his ears were unstopped and he heard that the Infinite Healing Intelligence responded to man's thought, that its Nature was responsive. His son had a healing.

The man felt the truth of what he affirmed. He tasted the sweet savor of God, meaning he had a delightful sensation in seeing his prayer bring forth a wonderful healing. His sense of smell was fed, i.e., discernment. He separated the false beliefs and errors in his mind and arrived at the truth, a feeling of harmony and perfection for his son. The five thousand (erroneous thoughts) were truly fed in the spiritual and psychological meaning of the Bible.

To understand this wonderful drama is to realize that all suffering, sickness, pain, and lack are all lies; then you experience an extraordinary inner calm that results through seeing the truth about yourself. This man saw the lying thoughts in him. Some of these thoughts said to him that his son could not be healed, "He's too far gone now," It's hopeless," "Why bother?" "Others died with the same disease," etc.

I told him to look at that motley crew in his own mind and feed them with the knowledge that the Living Intelligence and Power which made his son's body could also heal it. He proceeded to look at all the deceitful, lying, stupid, ignorant, superstitious, fearful thoughts (people) in his mind saying to himself, "I am a slave and a serf to these thoughts; they are my master. I should be the master and in control of my own mind, bidding all my servants (thoughts) what to do." He decided to take charge, become the master of his household, and give meat to all the hungry states.

We begin to *feed the five thousand* when we begin to discipline the five senses. (We have covered that to some extent in chapter four when we discussed the woman with the five husbands. The meaning is really the same). The point of this story in chapter six is to teach you to change your level of consciousness, to rise higher. The person you are, the state of mind you possess, attracts the same situations, the same insoluble problems. If you change yourself, your whole life will change. You find that the things which upset you no longer have the same power over you. When you pray you go into a mountain with your disciples, meaning your attitudes and mental faculties are turned to spiritual and mental processes.

(5) *Whence shall we buy bread?* refers to the bread of heaven, the bread of the silence where we mentally eat of harmony, health, peace, and all good things. (7) *Philip answered him, Two hundred pennyworth of bread is not sufficient for them, that every one of them may take a little.* (8) *One of his disciples, Andrew, Simon Peter's brother, saith unto him,* (9) *There is a lad here,*

which hath five barley loaves, and two small fishes: but what are they among so many?

The term *lad* means Christ, or man awakening to the truth. Names, such as John, Peter, Christ, etc., mean states of consciousness. To say, "John wrote the Gospel," does not prove it. There is no historical proof, actually no one knows for certain who *John* was, whose name is appended to this Gospel. We do not know exactly when it was published. All this is really of no importance, for the simple reason the psychological truths of the Bible are as true today as they were two thousand years ago. When we come to this parable of the loaves and fishes, we do not look upon it as a historical event, but rather something that is happening all the time in all parts of the world.

Two hundred pennyworth of bread is the double-minded state and will not satisfy man. It represents the confused state or feeling of lack.

To call Andrew means to see the truth about your capacity to show forth God's eternal supply. The word *Andrew* means perception or seeing the truth about any situation. It means to live in the truth.

Philip is the persistence, and *Peter* is faith in God.

We have *five barley loaves* signifying the undisciplined senses and two small fishes, referring to idea and feeling, or the harmonious union of the conscious and subconscious mind in prayer.

(10) *And Jesus said, Make the men sit down. Now there was much grass in the place. So the men sat down, in number about five thousand. (11) And Jesus took the loaves; and when he had given thanks, he distributed to the disciples, and the disciples to them that were set down; and likewise of the fishes as much as they would. (12) When they were filled, he said unto his disciples, Gather up the fragments that remain, that nothing be lost. (13) Therefore they gathered them together, and filled twelve baskets with the fragments of the five barley loaves, which remained over and above unto them that had eaten.*

Make the men sit down means to adopt the receptive attitude of mind. All characters of this drama are within yourself. You are Jesus calling your faculties and attitudes of mind together in the attitude of prayer for the purpose of solving your problems. In this process you separate yourself psychologically from the world, from the power of the senses, and you begin to see the solution to your problem. You still the wheels of your mind, the five senses are turned inward, and all your faculties and thoughts are focused on God.

Let me illustrate how a young man, in our Tuesday classes on "The meaning of the Sacraments" multiplied the loaves and fishes. He had ulcers of the stomach, had very little food for his family, and was living on twenty-five dollars a week from unemployment insurance. He was involved in all his aches, pains, misery, and negative imagery. This young man learned about the Infinite Healing Presence within him; several times daily he stilled his mind, got quiet, and began to claim that God's river of Peace and Harmony was saturating every atom of his being. He was focused on his health, had mental pictures of himself doing the things he always did, and eating the food he always ate. He was contemplating health and giving his devotion and attention to his highest concept of health. In his meditation he called Andrew by imagining his wife was congratulating him on his perfect health, his wonderful promotion, and added income. He performed this mental and spiritual operation frequently, which is calling Philip, meaning perseverance. He also called Peter, or faith, by having a conviction, a certainty, that the God-Presence was within; as a consequence he felt the health, abundance, and supply he needed was a definite possibility as the "nature of God or Infinite Intelligence is Responsiveness," as Troward says.

This kind of mental practice led him away from the confusion, vexations, and turmoil of his five senses into the quietness and acceptance of God's Healing Presence. He fed the five thousand unruly thoughts in his mind and multiplied his good by his knowledge of God and His laws.

Giving the five loaves to the disciples means that the five senses are now anointed with peace, harmony, and the sense of supply. Our senses are fed with the Inner Wisdom of God. You can practice feeding the five thousand now—today—as you read this. Move away from the cares and anxieties of the world; think of your Divine Centre; get the positive feeling that God is present there at that point of stillness. You are now breaking the hold of the fearful and warring five senses. Think of your desired objective, aims or goal, and know the hand of God is upon it. A stillness, an inner peace, and quietness will steal over you. As you adhere to the fact that through this Authority and Power of God you will receive an answer, you shall see a manifestation of your ideal.

Gathering up the fragments represents the Divine measure that is always "pressed down, shaken together, and running over." "Blessed are the merciful for they shall receive mercy."

To pray for another is to pray for yourself. To rejoice on the success of another is to bring success to yourself. Did you ever give some fragrant flowers to someone and then smell your hands? If so, you will remember the fragrant odor of your hands. The good you claim, feel, and believe as true of others will, of course, be resurrected in their experience, but you also will be blessed in countless ways, which means twelve basketsful are left over.

We will now give the highlights of the key passages or most important verses of the rest of this chapter.

(18) *And the sea arose by reason of a great wind that blew.* (19) *So when they had rowed about five and twenty or thirty furlongs, they see Jesus walking on the sea, and drawing nigh unto the ship: and they were afraid.* (20) *But he saith unto them, It is I; be not afraid.* (21) *Then they willingly received him into the ship: and immediately the ship was at the land whither they went.*

Entering a ship in biblical language is entering into a new mental attitude, mood, or feeling which transports you from one point in your mind to another, or higher level of consciousness. Jesus is always walking on the waters of your mind. *Jesus* is the idea or desire you seek, the solution to your problem. *The great wind that blew* represents the negative thoughts and emotional turmoil present in the individual. You may be saying at this moment, "I wish I could see the answer to my problem." That is Jesus coming down the waters of your mind.

Verse nineteen says they were afraid when they saw Jesus walking on the waters. Sometimes we are afraid to trust the Power within and we say, "I wish I knew the answer," or "There is no way out of this dilemma," etc. However, as we reflect on the truth we have been taught, we begin to realize the desire knocking at the door of our heart is just as real as any of the furnishings in the room we are in. It is real in another dimension of mind and has its own structure, form, and shape; but it seems intangible and invisible to us from a three-dimensional standpoint. The voice within you says, "It is I," meaning it is the Infinite One within you speaking to you saying your desire or idea is real, it is not a lie. The moment you realize your dream or ideal is real, you nourish it with attention, love, and devotion; then you are Jesus walking upon the waters of your own fear, hesitancy, and doubt. You stand on them, so to speak.

Your vision is now on your goal and you go where your wisdom is. Your faith and confidence are the ships which lead you to the port of safety. You are willingly receiving Jesus into your ship and *immediately the ship was at the land whither they went.* When you lose the sense of fear and walk with absolute confidence psychologically in your mind with your desire, you have accepted your savior; then Jesus has come into your ship. The *land* you arrive at is the manifestation of your goal.

(26) *Jesus answered them and said, verily, verily, I say unto you, Ye seek me, not because ye saw the miracles, but because ye did eat of the loaves, and were filled.* (27) *Labour not for the meat which perisheth, but for*

that meat which endureth unto everlasting life, which the Son of man shall give unto you: for him hath God the Father sealed.

The people seeking Jesus symbolize desires, ideas, and concepts that we have which are always tending toward fulfillment. We must seek the truth for its own sake and not just for the loaves and fishes. There is no real security in any tangible thing. There is no government that can legislate or guarantee peace, harmony, health, joy, abundance, and security. Our real security lies in our knowledge of God and our oneness with Him. The man who has an abiding faith and trust in God to supply all his needs will always be watched over by a benign Providence wherever he goes. When stock markets crash, governments topple, or when some natural calamity wipes away all his material possessions, the man of faith is always secure in God; his faith in the Divine Source is the rock on which he stands. It never fails him. He finds himself again living in the midst of God's abundance and peace.

Great material possessions, wealth, and lots of money are not a deterrent to spiritual growth or illumination, but while these things are necessary on this plane, we must know that our security does not rest in them. Our security is always in God and His love. When we place our trust in Him, we will in all probability suffer no material losses either, or if we do, we will recoup the losses immediately without suffering much discomfort in the meantime.

Peace, integrity, happiness, inspiration, and harmony are treasures of the spirit. They are intangible, and it is also well to remember that even though a man has a million dollars he cannot, for instance, buy health, peace, joy, or the real love of a woman. These are not for sale. The price we pay for the above qualities and attributes of God is faith, confidence, and trust in the Father of Lights, in whom there is no variableness, neither shadow of turning.

We must be friendly, not that we may gain friends, but because it is a God-given attribute to be friendly. Many people enter the Truth Movement, make a few demonstrations; then disappear only to return later when they are in trouble. We must seek the Truth for its own sake, and let all else go. Man abiding in the consciousness of peace, harmony, love, and realizing the availability of God's ideas and supply, never lacks for any good thing, for all things are added to him. Let us not labor for the meat which perisheth. *The meat which endureth forever* is the Divine ideas, the everlasting verities.

(30) *What sign shewest thou then, that we may see, and believe thee?*

Man is always looking for a sign. *There shall be no sign given him but the sign of Jonah,* which means one's inner feeling, our inner certitude or conviction in the reality of the invisible mental state in which we live, move, and have our being. We must learn to believe in the unseen; for "God calleth things that be not, as though they were, and the unseen becomes seen."

Some years ago I was told about a Scotch Presbyterian minister who was lost in the desert during the first world war. He took the Bible literally and asked that God send him manna. He received a sweet, sugary substance and ate of it. It was done unto him as he believed. However, flour, bread, cakes, etc. are not the true bread. *The true bread* is thoughts of peace, happiness, joy, and good will. When we identify ourselves with the great Truths of God, we are eating of the true bread of heaven.

(35) *And Jesus said unto them, I am the bread of life: he that cometh to me shall never hunger; and he that believeth on me shall never thirst.*

The bread you eat comes from heaven which is our own consciousness, or the Spiritual Power within us. You can enter the Secret Place now in your own mind, and feast on all good things. When you feast on the good things within, you shall never want for any good things on the external plane. The *banquet table* of the Lord or the Law is ever before us. *The bread* we eat is the Divine ideas; the meat we eat is Power and Strength of God; *the wine* we drink is the joyous feeling; *the fruit* is the answered prayer. When man discovers the Spiritual Power within he exclaims, "The wilderness is paradise now!"

Referring to the allegorical manna or heavenly food, the bread which the Lord hath given you to eat, Philo writes, "Dost thou not see the food of the soul, what it is? It is the Logos (light, truth, Divine ideas) of God, like unto dew, encircling the whole of the soul on all sides, and suffering no part of it (the soul) to be without its share of the Logos." The spiritual manna is wisdom, which waters our mind and heart and puts sweetness and gladness into our mouths.

(32) *Moses gave you not that bread from heaven.*

When Moses fed the manna to the Israelites in the wilderness, that was not the spiritual food from the Spiritual Power within. *Moses gave the bread of heaven* in the Ten Commandments and other parts of the Bible attributed to him. Literally speaking, *manna* is the sap and juice of the flowering ash used in medicine. I used to eat it as a boy and enjoyed its taste immensely. (I have no reason to doubt the story of the Scotch minister who said this substance-like-manna came floating in the air so he could eat it. He was sustained by this mysterious food until he was rescued; yet, that is not the true bread.) We may eat of delicious food and have all the wealth we want plus all manner of worldly and tangible possessions; yet, we can become very hungry for peace, joy, health, happiness, love, and laughter. All these come from God within and must be appropriated in our consciousness through meditation and prayer. This is why we read in the Bible, (34) *Then said they unto him, Lord, evermore give us this bread.* This is your cry and the desire of all men everywhere.*

(44) *No man can come to me, except the Father which hath sent me draw him: and I will raise him up at the last day.*

We can experience nothing unless it is a part of our consciousness. In other words, our level of being, or consciousness, attracts to us all experiences, conditions, and events. We cannot escape from the contents of our mind unless we decide to change. Before the old can be destroyed something new must be accepted mentally. As we learn to change our mental pattern and imagery according to spiritual standards, we will enjoy new and wonderful experiences. The outer world is always a reflection of the inner world of the mind; for "as within, so without."

The last day refers to the time we die to all sense of limitation and frustration, we are then raised up, or spiritually awakened. Every day is the last day in the sense that our last, waking estimate of ourselves,

---

* Read chapter on "Give Us This Day Our Daily Bread" in *Traveling with God*.

as we fall into the deep of sleep every night, is the last mental picture. It is our last concept; when we believe it, it shall be resurrected or raised up as a condition, experience, or event.

(53) *Except ye eat the flesh of the Son of man, and drink his blood, ye have no life in you.**

Eating of the flesh and drinking of the blood sig-nify that we mentally appropriate and pour life into our desire by feeling the reality of it. Blood is life. We must, therefore, animate and make alive our idea, desire, plan, or purpose. There must be a union of the mind and the heart. As we do this, we are eating and drinking of our desire. Except we do this, we have no life. We are dead. We must be creative and cause our ideas to take form in our experiences because our state of consciousness resurrects and makes alive all that we believe and give consent to.

(63) *It is the spirit that quickeneth; the flesh profiteth nothing: the words that I speak unto you, they are spirit, and they are life.*

Here Jesus explains that he is speaking psycholog-ically and not in a literal sense. To take the terms *flesh and blood* literally is, of course, too absurd for words. It is true that all food solid or liquid which we partake of is transmuted into tissue, muscle, bone, and blood

---

* See chapter on Holy Communion in my book *Prayer Is the Answer.*

cells; in that sense, all food undergoes transformation into the body and blood of God. The food eaten is also transformed into energy, circulating in our brain which is our thinking center. This is why one scientist said, some time ago, that the food we eat becomes a thought in the brain.

(70) *Have not I chosen you twelve, and one of you is a devil? Our devil* is our limitation. Our desire indicates our lack.

A brilliant artist in one of our classes pointed out that he could not bring out the really true tones, shades, and values of a brilliant color unless he used a background of gray and black. These latter shades seemed to enhance the beauty of the other.

How would you know what joy was unless you could shed a tear of sorrow? How could you know what peace was unless you could experience a twinge of pain? Man would not know what abundance was unless he could experience the sense of lack. All of us are born with twelve faculties; one of these is called Judas which means a sense of limitation. I must know I am in a sense of loss and privation before I can ever know what will fulfill my sense of lack.

Perhaps, as you read these pages, you have certain urges and desires for something grander and greater. You could not have these urges within you except for the fact that your present state is one of limitation. All of this is good. It is through our problems we grow. Every time you are presented with a difficulty or a problem, it is your opportunity to bring forth the Divinity within and conquer. You are born to conquer. If you had nothing to overcome, you would never discover yourself. You would be a robot. Your devil is the fact that you have left the absolute or unconditioned state and you now find yourselves in a conditioned or limited state which is called the three dimensional world.

(71) *He spake of Judas Iscariot the son of Simon: for he it was that should betray him, being one of the twelve.*

Judas interiorly symbolizes that state whence blossoms perfection. Your Judas is perhaps now reminding you that you desire a greater measure of health, a greater sense of freedom or abundance. Your state of lack prompts you, causes you to wish, and desire for fulfillment of these states of lack; hence Judas is betraying (revealing) your savior. The realization of your desire is always the savior, your salvation, your redeemer. This is why you can't dismiss Judas, as in the drama of the Bible Jesus (illumined reason) can't get rid of the man who betrays him. You can't possibly take this literally. It is beautiful and glorious when you understand the psychological and spiritual significance.

The Bible says that we will always have the poor with us. Of course, that is true. We must experience limitations in order to grow. There is no other way. When in bondage, you have the urge for freedom. Look around you in the field of electronics, chemistry, physics, astronomy, metaphysics, etc. We know very little even about electricity. Our knowledge of all these things is very limited. It is the same with everything. Do you say you know all there is to know about the hidden wisdom of the Bible? There are layers of meaning in the Bible which have not been plumbed by any man; in the same manner that there are fish in the sea that have never been seen nor caught. We are in the Presence of Infinity; never in Eternity could you exhaust the Glory and Beauty that is within you. All things are growing and unfolding in this world; there is nothing perfect.

The Book of Hebrews says that the works are finished and complete in the Absolute, or the Kingdom of God within. Your state of limitation, your problem, your difficulty is therefore a blessing in the sense that it is through these states of limitation you grow. As you grow in wisdom, you solve your problems. No matter how wise you are, whether a Paul, a Moses, or a Jesus, you will meet challenges and obstacles, for there is no end to spiritual growth and unfoldment. Being on the spiritual path, you will react differently to the challenges of the world. You will remain unmoved, undisturbed, calm, and peaceful because you have learned to turn all problems over to God and let Him carry the load. God wipes away all tears from your eyes, and there shall be no more crying.

By overcoming our problems through prayer and meditation, we reveal (betray) the Christ which means the Power of God in action. When we die completely to all sense of limitation, we become the God-man here and now returning to the glory which was ours before the world was. *Thou hast been in Eden, the garden of God; every precious stone was thy covering.* EZEKIEL 28:13.

Chapter 7

There is much repetition in this chapter. We will take the essential verses which reveal the most wonderful method of spiritual treatment ever given to man. The method of spiritual treatment outlined in the key verses of this chapter formed the basis of Quimby's amazing healings.

(1) *After these things Jesus walked in Galilee: for he would not walk in Jewry, because the Jews sought to kill him.* (2) *Now the Jews' feast of tabernacles was at hand.* (3) *His brethren therefore said unto him, Depart hence, and go into Judaea, that thy disciples also may see the works that thou doest.* (4) *For there is no man that doeth any thing in secret, and he himself seeketh to be known openly. If thou do these things, shew thyself to the world.* (5) *For neither did his brethren believe in him.* (6) *Then*

Jesus said unto them, My time is not yet come: but your time is always ready.

The brethren of Jesus are all those states of hope, faith, trust, desire, and ideals; these are always with us. We must be careful where we walk in our mind, in the same manner as we must be careful of where we walk on the outside. We must be extremely cautious of the company we keep as we walk down the streets of our mind. There are thoughts in your mind always seeking to kill your Jesus, or your desire.

You may desire health, this is Jesus walking in Galilee (your mind); other thoughts come and challenge you. They say, "You don't know enough," "You are getting worse," "What is the use," etc. You see these thoughts are about to slay your idea or desire for health. You must not permit them. You must subjectify your desire or idea of health by taking a vacation from the belief of the senses, detaching your attention from sickness and symptoms, and focusing your thoughts on the concept of health. As you make a habit of this by frequent occupancy of the mind with mental pictures of health, plus your belief in the response of the Healing Principle, you will succeed in going to Judea, i.e., the subconscious realization of perfect health.

The disciples you take with you in meditation are your faculties and attitudes turned inward toward the Divine Healing Presence. (6) *My time is not yet come;*

but your time is always ready. Your time has come when you have achieved victory over the problems or when a conviction has been reached. Faith, belief, and trust are always ready and waiting to work for you; these are your brethren.

In the following lies the key to the whole chapter, (33) *Then said Jesus unto them, Yet a little while am I with you, and then I go unto him that sent me. (34) Ye shall seek me, and shall not find me: and where I am, thither ye cannot come.*

What manner of saying is this that he said, "Ye shall seek me, and shall not find me: and where I am, thither ye cannot come?" Quimby said that the practical application of the principle of healing is outlined in these verses. This teacher of truth called in a woman who was aged, lame, bound down, and on crutches. He states that her ailment was due to the fact she was imprisoned by a creed so small and contracted that she could not stand upright or move ahead. She was living in the tomb of fear and ignorance; furthermore, she was taking the Bible literally and it frightened her. In this tomb, Quimby said, was the Presence of God trying to burst the bars, break through the bands, and rise from the dead. When she would ask others for an explanation of some passage of the Bible, the answer would be a stone; then she would hunger for the bread of life. Dr. Quimby diagnosed her case as a mind cloudy and stagnated due to excitation and fear caused by inability to see clearly the meaning of the Scriptural passages she had been reading. This showed itself in the body by her heavy and sluggish feeling which would terminate in paralysis.

Here at this point Quimby asked her what was meant, *A little while I am with you and then I go to him that sent me.* She replied it meant that Jesus went to heaven. Quimby explained what it really meant by explaining that *being with her a little while* meant his explanation of her symptoms, feelings, and their cause; i.e., he had compassion and sympathy for her momentarily, but he could not remain in that mental state; the next step was to go to Him that sent us, which is the Presence of God in all of us.

Quimby immediately traveled in his mind and contemplated perfect health, which is a part of God. He said to the woman we are talking about, "Therefore where I go, you cannot come, for you are in Calvin's belief, and I am in health." This explanation produced an instantaneous sensation, and a change came over her mind. She walked without her crutches. She was, as it were, dead in error, and to bring her to life or truth was to raise her from the dead. "I quoted the resurrection of Christ and applied it to her own Christ or health; it produced a powerful effect on her." (Quimby's *Manuscripts.*)

Apply this principle of healing in your life. Supposing your son is sick, go within to Him who sent you. God or Life, sent all of us into the World. God is all Bliss, Harmony, Peace, Beauty, Wisdom, and Perfection. You turn within in thought and quietly realize that the Wisdom and Infinite Intelligence of God is right there within you. The Living Intelligence and Power of God sent you into this world and fashioned all your organs from its own Invisible Pattern. You are now turning to the maker of your body. You are relaxed, at peace, poised, and calm. You are full of confidence that the Creator of your body and mind can create and refashion your body according to His Own Divine Pattern.

You have seen your son, sick and in pain, but now in your meditation you are talking to the God-Presence calling forth its Healing Presence. Think of your son and immediately dwell on the peace, health, and harmony of God. You know these qualities, potencies, and aspects of God are now being reflected in your boy. You are now getting into the mental atmosphere of health and, like Quimby, you are contemplating the Divine ideal which is perfection, wholeness, and harmony for your son. Do it frequently three or four times daily until you believe in the idea of perfect health. When you mentally accept that the Healing Power of God is working for your son, that is a treatment.

You will seek me and you cannot find me means others may wonder what you are doing and be unable to follow you in understanding or belief. *And where I am, thither ye cannot come.* Other members of the family or the patient himself may be unable to rise in consciousness and enter into the feeling of perfect health because they are wrapped up in worldly beliefs. Quimby said that man's false belief was the sepulcher in which the Wisdom of God is confined, and that the truth is the angel which rolled away the stone of superstition and ignorance healing the mind and body.

The word *treatment* used in New Thought circles means the harmonious interaction and direction of the conscious and subconscious powers for a definite, specific purpose. In treating others or ourselves we never identify with the disease. We have compassion for the person momentarily, *yet a little while I am with you*; then we go to God and Heaven realizing the ideal perfection of the patient. The pharisaical beliefs (fear and doubt) cannot enter where confidence in God's Power is. In prayer you are one with God, the only Presence and Power.

(42) *Christ cometh of the seed of David, and out of the town of Bethlehem, where David was?*

Christ, or the Spirit of Truth, comes out of Bethlehem—house of bread, our own consciousness, or awareness—called I AM. Quimby called Christ,

"Wisdom." We must look for Wisdom within. To know that you can embrace an idea, emotionalize it, and feel its reality causing it to become manifest on the screen of space is a part of the Wisdom called Christ. To know that you are what you think all day long is also a part of the Wisdom called Christ.

(49) *But this people who knoweth not the law are cursed.*

When we make a negative use of the law we experience the automatic response which is, of course, negative. This is called a curse in the Bible. It is wisdom to know that "as a man thinketh in his heart so is he." *Get wisdom and with all thy getting, get understanding.* Prov. 4:7.

Chapter 8

(1) Jesus went unto the mount of Olives. (2) And early in the morning he came again into the temple, and all the people came unto him; and he sat down, and taught them. (3) And the scribes and Pharisees brought unto him a woman taken in adultery; and when they had set her in the midst, (4) They say unto him, Master, this woman was taken in adultery, in the very act. (5) Now Moses in the law commanded us, that such should be stoned: but what sayest thou? (6) This they said, tempting him, that they might have to accuse him. But Jesus stooped down, and with his finger wrote on the ground, as though he heard them not. (7) So when they continued asking him, he lifted up himself, and said unto them, He that is without sin among you, let him first cast a stone at her. (8) And again he stooped down, and wrote on the ground. (9) And they which heard it, being convicted by their own conscience, went out one by one, beginning at the eldest, even unto the last: and Jesus was left alone, and the woman standing in the midst. (10) When Jesus had lifted up

himself, and saw none but the woman, he said unto her, Woman, where are those thine accusers? hath no man condemned thee? (11) She said, No man, Lord. And Jesus said unto her, Neither do I condemn thee: go, and sin no more. (12) Then spake Jesus again unto them, saying, I am the light of the world: he that followeth me shall not walk in darkness, but shall have the light of life.

Jesus *going up the mount of Olives* means spiritual understanding. When you turn within to the God-Presence seeking light on your problem, peace, truth, and beauty minister unto you. People are prone to take everything literally. We must remember there is an allegory of words also. For example, when we speak of the blind, the halt, the deaf, and the lame, we must remember there is a spiritual blindness, an inner deafness, although the outer ears are normal and not diseased. There are those who do not want to hear anything new. They refuse to listen to the psychological meaning of the Bible and they are spiritually deaf. Many people are afraid to move forward to their announced goal; they see obstacles; these are lame people.

The idea behind all Bible stories is to convey a psychological and higher meaning than that of the literal interpretations of the words. To look at this parable literally is one thing, to understand it from a psychological standpoint is another. Quimby, about one hundred years ago, gave the interpretation of the woman caught in adultery. I think his insight into the meaning of this parable is superb. He points out that the adultery spoken of in those days was that she left the old orthodox ways and began to listen to the teachings of Jesus. She had, therefore, sinned in the eyes of all her former friends. The stones represented the accusations, ridicule, and abuse heaped on her by others; however, when she ceased to worry about what others thought, and as she adhered to the truth, she ceased to find fault with herself. When she ceased to find fault with herself, all the world ceased to throw stones at her!

This means that no matter how a man may have transgressed the laws of life, no matter how heinous his crime, even though he is condemned by society; if he will rise in consciousness to the point where he ceases to condemn himself, the tongues of all the gossips are stilled and not a hand is lifted against him. A few perfunctory prayers will not suffice, but a deep hunger and thirst to become a new man, plus a transformation of the mind and heart, will expunge from the mind the errors of the past and make all things new. *Though your sins be scarlet, they shall be white as snow, though red like crimson they shall be as wool.*

The word *adultery* spoken of in the Bible means idolatry or spiritual immorality. Whenever we enter into a negative mood of fear, hate, and resentment, we have committed adultery because we have married a false belief and adulterated the truth. Whenever we believe in two powers, or if we say there is a devil, we are committing adultery in the real meaning of the word. Any time we cohabit with evil, such as envy, jealousy, slander, criticism, resentment, hate, etc., we are polluting the sanctuary of God, which is our own mind.

It is written that our mind should be called a house of prayer, but when we identify with negative thoughts and emotions, we make our mind a den of thieves. Whatever we are identified with, we become. If we identify with resentment we have committed adultery in the heart (subjective feeling, emotion); this negative emotion now governs and controls our speech, thought, actions, and reactions. When man is under the sway of negative imagery and emotion, he is a serf or a slave, and is being actually ordered around like a servant by the negative thoughts reigning supreme in his mind. (I would refer you, at this time, to the second chapter "Marriage Feast of Cana" where it is pointed out that all prayer is really a marriage feast.)

What are you mentally and emotionally identified with at this moment? Your marriage partner is your present feeling, awareness, mood, or inner conviction. Your estimate or blueprint of yourself determines what kind the children of your mind will be. The children which come forth from your real feeling about yourself are made manifest as health, peace, abundance, social, and financial status, etc. Any time you give attention, feeling, and emotion to any negative thought or idea, you are committing adultery in Biblical language.

If a wife or husband begins to brood or nourish a grudge, he or she has already committed adultery, because this person is mentally and emotionally united with ideas and concepts of a negative nature. The man who is crotchety, petulant, cantankerous, and constantly complaining is cohabiting and lying down with evil thoughts in his bed. *His bed* means his mind. We lie down amidst our thoughts, don't we? Do we find rest unto our soul? We would find that deep abiding peace, rest, stillness, and security if we returned in thought and love to the Divine Center within and looked at others through the light of our aim. *Our aim* is peace, harmony, joy, health, and happiness.

Begin now to reach toward everyone according to the Eternal Verities. You will find yourself under the influence of the spiritual forces within you. Whenever you feel yourself prone to be angry, think immediately of your aim, goal or objective in life; immediately all the force is taken away from the negative thought. A positive, confident feeling of goodness, truth, and beauty will take over, and you go ahead spiritually by leaps and bounds.

(5) *Now, Moses in the law commanded us, that such should be stoned.*

Begin now to see the psychological significance of this wonderful drama. Notice how people throw stones at themselves all day long. Take, for instance, a man who lost considerable money in business; let us say he went into bankruptcy; oftentimes he sits alone, broods, criticizes, castigates, and flagellates himself saying, "Why did you invest that money?" "You should have known you would fail," "I'm no good," "I'm a failure," and a dozen other statements of a similar nature flow silently from his lips. He is accusing himself. He is throwing stones at himself. The only accuser is the feeling of lack, failure, and inability to realize our objective.

The harlot, the woman with the illegitimate child, who may be condemned and stoned by the world, may turn to the truth within and claim her freedom.

She realizes that God condemns no one. *His eyes are too pure to behold iniquity. Society and the world may condemn her. All judgment is given to the son. The son,* as Dr. Nicoll says, is your mind. This is the place you pronounce judgment on yourself by the thoughts you entertain. The harlot learns that all she has to do is to cease condemning herself; God has already forgiven her. As a matter of fact God or the Absolute knows nothing about her errors or fears. She, therefore, forgives herself by giving herself the mood of peace, love, and harmony for the mood of guilt, despair, and self-condemnation. She turns from the past and completely detaches herself from the former way of living. She mentally and emotionally identifies herself with her aim which is peace, dignity, happiness, and freedom. As she does, God and His Glory respond automatically. She finds a wave of peace moving over the arid areas of her mind like the dew of heaven; moreover, the Light of God penetrates all the dark corners of her mind. The dawn of God's Wisdom appears, and the shadows of fear, guilt, and self-condemnation flee away. As she ceases to condemn herself, neither can the world condemn her.

(10) *Hath no man condemned thee?* (11) *She said, No man, Lord.*

This parable states Jesus stooped down. We *stoop down* whenever we turn away from the One Presence and Power and worship false gods. We must never descend from our high state of consciousness. We must never be deflected from our aim. When we permit fear, worry, and anxiety to enter in, we have stooped down or turned away from faith in God and all things good.

The devil represents the accuser in the Bible, or the negative thoughts and feelings we entertain which remind us that we have missed the mark or our objective in life. Remind yourself of God, remember Him, and go back to the Source from which you came; think, speak, and act from the Divine Center within you which is the Secret Place of the Most High; you will then be lifted up and again be identified with your aims which are the great Truths of God which you have learned. You are here primarily to resurrect God's qualities. When you mentally think of Him and His Love, you are always lifting yourself up into a higher level of being.

(7) *He lifted himself, and said unto them, He that is without sin among you, let him first cast a stone at her.*

This is exactly the way you address the motley crew in your mind. You silence them by completely rejecting them mentally, realizing they have no power—nothing to sustain them. They are nothing trying to be something. You chop their heads off, cremate, and burn them up because you have returned in faith and confidence to the Secret Place of Stillness within yourself, where God and His Omnipotence dwells. The armor of God is around you now.

(9) *Jesus was left alone, and the woman standing in the midst . . .*

Jesus and the woman represent yourself when you have actually united with what you want to be or to have. All condemnation is gone. You are alone with your ideal. You have experienced the joy of the answered prayer in your own heart.

There is much repetition in the rest of this eighth chapter of John. We will, however cast light on the main or most important verses.

(24) *If ye believe not that I am he, ye shall die in your sins.*

Troward says, "I am that which I contemplate." You become what you claim and feel yourself to be. Except you now believe and accept as true that you now are what you long to be, you will remain as you are. In other words, you will *die in your sins,* meaning you will fail to reach your mark in life. If a man who is poverty-stricken refuses to enter into the mood of opulence and the belief in a God of abundance forever supplying all his needs, he will remain poor regardless of the church he joins or what creed he adopts.

(31) *If ye continue in my word, then are ye my disciples indeed; (32) and ye shall know the truth, and the truth shall make you free.*

One obvious truth is this, if you were now sick, the realization of health and peace of mind would free you; this would be the truth which would set you free. The acceptance of your desire for health would be your savior and redeemer. You continue in the word when you remain faithful to the idea or feeling of perfect health in your mind regardless of appearance. The *word* is your thought, your feeling, or inner awareness.

A few minutes ago, while writing this chapter, a woman telephoned me long distance telling me how she put into practice one of the healing methods outlined in one of my recent books *Traveling with God*. She had what the doctor said was a very severe case of blood poisoning in her foot which penicillin and other antibiotics failed to relieve. She was unable to walk. Six or seven times during the day she stilled the wheels of her mind, closed her eyes, and went within. She turned mentally away from the foot, the appearance of things, and became completely detached. Quietly and gently she claimed that the Infinite Healing Presence was saturating every thought and every atom of her being making her whole, pure, and perfect. She kept affirming this for two or three minutes. In her imagination she walked around the house sensing and feeling all the objects in the house, and doing all the things she ordinarily would do. She did this for about five minutes; then she ended her spiritual treatment by giving thanks to the God-Presence within. She sustained this method of prayer for several days (she continued in the word) until a complete healing took place. The day the doctor was supposed to operate on her he was amazed at the complete, rapid healing of her foot.

The *knowing of the truth* is simply a movement of your mind whereby you identify with your desire, accepting it completely. Maybe you are saying to yourself, "I wish I could get out of this present position." Or maybe someone reading this is saying, "I wish I could go to London for a vacation but I have no money." You are free because you can shut out your present surroundings and mentally feel and imagine you are in London. You can remain in this meditative state for several minutes or longer until you feel the naturalness of the state. As you open your eyes, you are not in London, but you traveled there psychologically. You fixed it in your mind. You have freed yourself from your sense of want or lack. The Deeper Self will devise the way whereby you will go to London. You can mentally appropriate and take possession of any state of consciousness; this is why you are free. Your state of consciousness objectifies your meditations, feelings, and beliefs.

(44) *Ye are of your father the devil, and the lusts of your father ye will do.*

If we have a negative idea enthroned in the mind, our father is the devil. We must impregnate our mind with the seeds of truth and nourish their gestation with love and devotion. If a man is hateful or resentful, he has evil for his father and his mother. The dominant mood is always the controlling factor. Belief in fear, old age, death, sickness, and all other false beliefs represent the devil, because they lie about the truth. When you spell devil backwards, it spells *lived*. Millions of people are governed by the thoughts of the past and are living according to the old pattern and experience. In other words, they are living backwards, because they are being ruled by doubts and fears acquired in the past. The *devil* means living backwards.

(58) *Before Abraham was, I am.*

Before any manifestation appears, it must first come out of the invisible. We must first have the feeling of conviction in our own consciousness. Where were you before you were born? You are told in plain language you were in the I AM state. You were in the Absolute or Paradisaical State. When your boy or girl is born, the child is the Universal Life, God, or I AM assuming the role of that particular child. It is the Unconditioned becoming conditioned. It is the Formless taking form. *I was naked and ye clothed me.*

Chapter 9

(1) And as Jesus passed by, he saw a man which was blind from his birth. (2) And his disciples asked him, saying Master, who did sin, this man, or his parents, that he was born blind? (3) Jesus answered, Neither hath this man sinned, nor his parents: but that the works of God should be made manifest in him. (4) I must work the works of him that sent me, while it is day: the night cometh, when no man can work. (5) As long as I am in the world, I am the light of the world. (6) When he had thus spoken, he spat on the ground, and made clay of the spittle, and he anointed the eyes of the blind man with the clay. (7) And said unto him, Go, wash in the pool of Siloam (which is by interpretation, Sent.) He went his way therefore, and washed, and came seeing. (8) The neighbours therefore, and they which before had seen him that he was blind, said, Is not this he that sat and begged? (9) Some said, This is he: others said, He is like him: but he said, I am he.

Here we are told the story of a man born blind, and the usual question is asked, "Who did sin, this man or his parents?" In a spiritual sense all men are born blind when born into this three dimensional plane. We have left the formless state and we look upon the world and see the limitation and restriction, having lost the awareness of our dominion and power over external circumstances and conditions. *Our birth* is called the fall of man, and our awakening to the Power of God within us is called being born again. When we are possessed by wisdom, we begin to see spiritually. Man is psychologically and spiritually blind when he does not know that he becomes what he thinks all day long. Emerson said, "A man is what he thinks all day long." The Bible says, "As a man thinketh in his heart, so is he."

Man is spiritually blind when he hates, resents, or is envious of others. He does not know he is actually secreting mental poisons which tend to destroy himself. If you say there is no way to solve this problem, that the situation is hopeless, that is spiritual blindness. You begin to *see* when you get a new perception of the mind knowing that there is an Infinite Intelligence within you which can solve all problems and which responds to your thought. Your mind has now received a new illumination, a new light. As you mentally claim that God is guiding you now, revealing to you the perfect answer, you find yourself automatically led to do the right thing and the way opens up. You were once blind to these truths; now you begin to see the vision of your health, wealth, happiness, and peace of mind.

Looking at the story of the Bible in another way, it was believed in the old days that if a man were born blind, it was due to past karma and that he was here to expiate for his sins. The people of that day also believed that the sins of the parents were communicated to the children. For example, if the parents were insane, all their children would be insane also. Troward says, "If a thing is true, there is a way in which it is true."

The *sin* spoken of in the Bible refers to the mental attitude, the mood, the feeling of the parents. All sin refers to movements of the mind rather than that of the body. Parents transmit their habitual thinking, their fear, tensions, and false beliefs to their children through the mind, not the body. Our feelings and moods create. What is the nature of your mood? What tone do you strike during the marital, creative act?*

---

* See chapter four in my book *Meaning of Reincarnation*.

For example, if there is someone in the parents' world whom they hate the sight of, or if there is a voice that they wish they would not hear again, a corresponding expression is brought forth. There are blind and deaf states of consciousness from which blind and deaf children come forth. Whatever tone is struck by the parents, a corresponding expression comes forth by the laws of reciprocal relationship.

In Ezekiel is written, *What mean ye, that ye use this proverb concerning the land of Israel, saying, The fathers have eaten sour grapes, and the children's teeth are set on edge? As I live, saith the Lord God, ye shall not have occasion any more to use this proverb in Israel.* Ezek. 18:2–3.

The only thing passed on to children are the moods, mental states, or beliefs of the parents. It is possible, for instance, for anyone to have a son who may become a Shakespeare, Beethoven, Lincoln, or a Jesus depending on the moods of the parents or their state of consciousness at the moment of conception. Jesus or Illumined Reason rejects the popular, superstitious belief of the people that the man's blindness was due to his karma. That is to say, he may have blinded people in a former life and is now back on this plane again to suffer and atone for his crime. Another very popular, superstitious belief was and still is that he was born blind because his parents were blind, or they had sinned or had some physical disease. Of course, as you know, a man and wife though congenitally blind or blinded by accident may give birth to children with perfectly normal vision.

It is the mood or state of consciousness at the moment of conception during the marital, creative act which determines the nature of the child. It is also true that a mother through prayer, may change the mental and physical nature of her child while he is still in the womb. A mother through prayer could bring about a perfect healing. In God's eyes the child is perfect. God sees all His creations as Infinite Perfection.

The answer of the man of prayer or the scientific thinker to all disease and trouble is to set forth the works of God, "I must work the works of him that sent me, while it is day." This means while the Light of Truth is shining, we consciously direct the law. A great number of people have healed their eyes through prayer. The Absolute never condemns or judges.

You can read in various magazine articles the miracles of healing taking place at various shrines throughout the world, setting forth the Power of the Healing Presence within all of us Which never fails to respond, as we turn to It in faith and trust. It is never the shrine, the ritual, or ceremony which heals, it is faith which makes them whole. The voodoo doctor in the jungles of Africa and Australia heals by faith also.

There are others who claim they are healed by bathing in certain waters or pools and by the bones of saints which they have touched. The reason for these healings is that their minds moved from fear and worry to faith.

There is no understanding behind these blind, faith healings. All these methods are good inasmuch as they relieve man of his troubles, pain, and sickness; however relapse is frequent because there is no scientific awareness of the Spiritual Power involved, and many return to the old, mental patterns reinfecting themselves as before. Scientific, Divine healing is the combined function of the conscious and subconscious powers directed specifically and scientifically for a definite purpose. The *works of the Father* are to express His own Nature, Goodness, Truth, and Beauty for He is within us.

To make clay of the spittle represents a drooling state like a boy hungers for candy and drools at the mouth. It is that joyful, bubbling up state. You have seen geysers bubbling up; the clay is very much alive. The clay represents the average man who is dead and unaware of the treasure-house within him. He is dead to his inner potentialities being unaware of the Presence and Power of God within him. As he awakens and becomes enthused, he becomes alive to God; this is the meaning of *he spat on the ground and made clay of the spittle.* This latter phrase is an oriental, idiomatic, figurative expression meaning a deep, inner conviction that we now have in consciousness what we want and we reject blindness or the old state of limitation. We now see the truth in the same way a boy sees the answer on the blackboard to his problem in trigonometry.

For example, a boy may write down on the blackboard three and three equals seven. The teacher is absolutely sure, based on his knowledge of the science of mathematics, that three plus three equals six. His declaration or pronouncement that three and three are six does not make it so; it always was so. He is convinced of its truth, consequently the boy rearranges his figures on the blackboard to conform to the truth.

Likewise, what is true of God is true of man. God can't possibly be blind, deaf, dumb, or sick. The truth about man is that the Living Spirit Almighty is within him. It is all Bliss, Wholeness, Joy, Perfection, Harmony, and Peace. It is all the wonderful things you have ever heard of. There cannot possibly be any quarrel or division in this Boundless Wisdom. Therefore, as you anchor your mind on these Eternal Truths about God, identifying yourself with them mentally, a rearrangement of the thought-pattern takes place in your mind and the Wholeness and Perfection of God is made manifest. The boy had to rearrange his figures to conform to the mathematical principle in the same manner as you redirected your thought-pattern in accordance with the principle of harmony. The electrons of your body automatically respond in accordance with the law of reciprocal relationship or the law of correspondence. *The clay* spoken of is a hard, dry, false belief. It is a muddy, confused mind which must be cleansed; then we spit (bring) forth our conviction of truth.

Go wash in the pool of Siloam means give up, send away. We are now detaching our consciousness from the old state which washes away the false idea and we feel and affirm the spirituality of all substance. The blind state also represents our inability to see the state that would bless us. When man does not know that his savior is the realization of his heart's desire, he is truly blind.

Had I not come they would not have known sin. In the blind state we do not know sin even though we may manifest lack and limitation of all kinds. The race-mind is doing all our thinking for us, for when our eyes are opened, we begin to think for ourselves. We think from the Divine Center within; therefore we no longer think negatively, but positively. As long as we continue to think from the artificial, superimposed centers of prejudice, fear, and ignorance, we shall experience strife, sickness, and violence. Let us be true thinkers and we shall experience mercy which droppeth as the gentle rain from heaven.

To sin is to miss the target of peace, health, and happiness. It is our failure to reach our goal or objective in life. If we have no mark to shoot at, we certainly do not sin. The real sin is failure to realize our objective and live a full and happy life.

There is much repetition in the rest of the chapter, but we will take the key verses, or the main highlights, and elucidate on them.

(14) *And it was the sabbath day when Jesus made the clay, and opened his eyes.* (15) *Then again the Pharisees also asked him how he had received his sight.*

The Pharisee is everywhere. He is the five-sense man or the man who adheres to ritual, ceremony, form, and external forms of worship. He thinks the sabbath refers to a day of the week and fails to realize that the sabbath is an inner movement and engagement of the mind on our ideal or desire, until we reach a point of stillness within and the outside world and its verdict no longer trouble us. We are alone with God and resting on our inner knowing. The Pharisee does not know where the solution is because he looks to the outside and not the inside. The inside is cause, the outer is effect. The Pharisee is always making the outside cause, worshipping the letter of the law and lacking the spirit which giveth life. When we awaken to our Inner Powers we exclaim, "Whereas I was blind, now I see."

(41) *If ye were blind, ye should have no sin: but now ye say, We see; therefore your sin remaineth.*

Pharisaical thoughts come into the mind of all of us at times when we pray, namely the doctrines, opinions, and teachings of men. The questioning and apparent argument that follow from verse eighteen to the end of the chapter represent those states of consciousness concerned only with form, ritual, and ceremonies. The practice of religion to the average Pharisee who is walking the streets of every city in the world is based upon adherence to tradition and superstition. To open the eyes of the blind, or the healing of a cancerous condition through prayer seems impossible to these people for they believe in the verdict of the race mind and world-opinion only.

We must look through the symbol of religion and see the principle behind it. The latter is the meaning of the phrase, (39) *For judgement I am come into this world, that they which see not might see; and that they which see might be made blind.* You are here to judge, for all judgment is given to the son. Your thought is the judge, to think is to compare. You compare one thing with another. You accept the good and reject the negative or false belief. You are here to discern, discriminate, and choose. When you discover God within, you choose only from the treasure-house of God's riches. You are awakening to the truth. Prior to that you did not know how to choose. Now your knowledge and awareness of the Divine Power enable you to choose only that which heals, elevates, blesses, and enriches you.

If you had real free will, you would not choose sickness, lack, misery, pain, and misfortune. *That they which see not might be made blind . . .* When functioning as a five-sense-man, living like most people in the law of averages, you must become blind to all your former theories, beliefs, traditions, and dogma and become alive to God and His Omnipotence; then you truly see. In the true process of prayer you must become deaf and blind to anything and everything that challenges your prayer. You refuse to look at evidence of things and appearances. Your vision is on God and His answer. If we have no target to shoot at, we do not miss it or sin, but if we claim to know the truth and fail to realize our objective, our sin remaineth. It is not enough to say, "I see the truth;" we must know the truth, and the truth will set us free. *Knowing* is the inner seeing or silent inner conviction wherein we raise the idea or desire to the point of acceptance. Herein lies our freedom.

Chapter 10

(1) Verily, verily, I say unto you, He that entereth not by the door into the sheepfold, but climbeth up some other way, the same is a thief and a robber. (2) But he that entereth in by the door is the shepherd of the sheep. (3) To him the porter openeth; and the sheep hear his voice: and he calleth his own sheep by name, and leadeth them out. (4) And when he putteth forth his own sheep, he goeth before them, and the sheep follow him: for they know his voice. (5) And a stranger will they not follow, but will flee from him: for they know not the voice of strangers. (6) This parable spake Jesus unto them: but they understood not what things they were which he spake unto them. (7) Then said Jesus unto them again, Verily, verily, I say unto you, I am the door of the sheep. (8) All that ever came before me are thieves and robbers: but the sheep did not hear them. (9) I am the door: by me if any man enter in, he shall be saved, and shall go in and out, and find pasture. (10) The thief cometh not, but for to steal, and to

*kill, and to destroy: I am come that they might
have life, and that they might have it more abun-
dantly.*

The *door* is the door of our own consciousness. *I
am the door.* Everything we experience in life comes
through our own consciousness. Our states of consciousness represent what we think, feel, believe,
and give consent to. Our states of consciousness are
always made manifest. Nothing happens on the outside without first happening on the inside. Before we
can manifest health, peace, and abundance, we must
first possess our desire in consciousness. We must
have the feeling of possession inside. I must be before
I can have. The ancients said, "To be is to have."

If a man tries to achieve what he wants through
external means, it will forever elude him. He is a thief
and a robber in the sense that he is robbing himself of
the joy of manifesting his ideal, by refusing to claim
and feel its reality mentally. He must have the mental
equivalent first; then its manifestation follows. Our
own mind or consciousness is the door to all expression. I talk to people who are trying to be spiritual
by going on rigid diets, abstaining from certain plea-

sures, and subjecting the body to very difficult and painful postures. Others go on fruit diets and retire from life, hoping that by this means they will reach higher levels of development. Fasting and going on rigid, physical discipline will not bring about a mental transformation which is what is desired. They are trying to climb some other way, and, of course they become completely disillusioned.

It is absurd to imagine or conceive that a person starting from the external standpoint could reach higher levels of spiritual awareness. The alibi such people use is that it is written, "A man must deny himself." You must deny yourself the morbid satisfaction of entertaining grudges, pet peeves, ill will, resentment, self-righteousness, spiritual pride, self-justification, and holier than thou attitudes. The above mentioned passage quoted by some people must be seen in its true psychological light to have any meaning at all. It surely does not mean that you deny yourself the comforts and conveniences of life. Where did these things come from? You must deny and reject the old way of thinking and reacting before you can possibly rise to higher levels. You cannot remain the same mentally and ascend spiritually. There must be an internal change. *Be not conformed to this world: but be ye transformed by the renewing of your mind.* ROM. 12:2.

You have noticed, or at least you are aware of the metamorphosis of the grubworm out of a butterfly. This symbolizes a transformation which you can undergo. You have wings which have not been used, the ways of thought and feeling, enabling you to soar aloft into the bosom of your Father in heaven. The transformation in Biblical language does not refer to the transformation of a cell into a human being, but refers to a psychological and an emotional change.

Let us take the following simple illustration: A man wishes to be healed and affirms over and over, "I am healed." If his statements are mechanical, he will get no results. He must enter into the spirit or feeling of perfect health. He must claim and feel the truth of what he affirms in consciousness. Healing follows the silent inner knowing of the soul. To be wealthy I must assume the consciousness of wealth; then wealth will follow. If you want to grow spiritually, there is a wonderful standard set up by Paul, *Whatsoever things are honest, whatsoever things are just, whatsoever things are pure, whatsoever things are lovely, whatsoever things are of good report; if there be any virtue, and if there be any praise, think on these things.* Phil. 4:8.

Start from within—not from without, spiritualize your thoughts, feelings, reactions, and emotions. See to it that all your thoughts, mental practices, and impulses conform to the spiritual standard of Paul.

The outside will correspond with the inside. The thieves and robbers are the negative thoughts and emotions in which we indulge. Fear, ignorance, and superstition are real thieves. They rob us of health, happiness, and peace of mind.

The *sheep* mentioned in this chapter are the noble, wonderful, dignified states of consciousness that bless us. Our conviction and understanding of the good is the shepherd who watches over our sheep (mental state). The dominant state of mind always rules and governs in the same manner as a general commands in the army. We become the true shepherd when we know the creative power and authority of our own mind. We have confidence and trust in our ability to choose the good and to reject mental food which is unsavory. We *call our sheep by name* when we enter into the feeling of having, being, or doing the things we long to have, be, or do. If we sustain these moods, they jell and crystallize within us, and those subjectified embodiments become objectified manifestations.

In verse four we are really instructed in the law of mental equivalents, meaning that we must mentally accept and feel the truth of what we affirm prior to its manifestation. In other words, feeling precedes all manifestation. As Judge Troward says, "Feeling is the law and the law is the feeling." The voice is the mood, tone, or mental attitude. Conditions, circumstances, and events follow the inner mental mood of man. Quimby said, "Man is belief expressed."

The voice of the stranger is to claim one thing and feel another. For instance, a man may pray for a healing and believe that he is incurable or that the stars are against him. Such an attitude of mind is like mixing an acid with alkali, you get an inert substance. There is an answer, of course, in the lack of what we pray for. If a man claims to be other than he really feels himself to be, he is robbing himself. He may claim to be a great actor and at the same time he knows in his heart he is not; such a man is a thief and a robber. The sheep (the embodied lovely states) will not follow such a negative attitude. *Sheep* are tended animals. Boasting and masquerading without the inner conviction fail to materialize. *All that ever came before me were thieves and robbers does* not mean, as some people claim, that all religions before Christianity were false. Such a statement is untrue and ridiculous.

I am sure the following interpretation makes sense. If you believe that circumstances, conditions, events, age, race, lack of money, etc. can preclude your possibility of realizing your objective, you are a thief and a robber for the simple reason you and you alone are robbing yourself of the joy of becoming what you long to be. There is only One Power, and your conviction regarding the answer to your prayer cannot be rescinded. "One with God is a majority." "If God be for you, who can be against you?" This is why it is said, "All that ever came before me are thieves and robbers."

In verse eleven it says, "The good shepherd giveth his life for the sheep." You must animate and make alive the desires of your heart. You must give them life by pouring life, love, and feeling upon your plans, goals, and objectives in life. The brain and the heart must be united as a wedded pair. Thought must be blended with emotion in order to embody your dreams.

In verse twelve the reference to *the wolf* means any mood of lack, doubt, and fear which neutralizes and destroys our positive ideals. We must retain an unassailable and unshakeable conviction in the good. If we do not do this, we are mere hirelings because we do not possess our sheep. We do not possess the idea in consciousness. We do not really believe even though we may intellectually accept.

(16) *And other sheep I have, which are not of this fold: them also I must bring, and they shall hear my voice; and there shall be one fold, and one shepherd.*

We have many desires or sheep, as well as one supreme and uppermost desire. A man may desire health and true expression, at the same time he may wish prosperity for his son, and a happy marriage for his daughter. To obtain these desires he will *treat each one specifically, specializing the law.* He does this by communing in the silence. When he has finished treating each one, he realizes that all the requests are now granted. His word (thought and feeling) is the law whereunto it is sent, and he goes off to sleep in the joyous conviction that all his prayers are answered. The *one fold* is the all embracing envelope or mood of love; *the one shepherd* is the absolute conviction it is so.

In verse seventeen *I lay down my life, that I might take it again,* refers to the fact that you must die to the old concept or estimate of yourself before you can resurrect your new ideal. Before something is born, something must die. The materialistic-minded man must die before the spiritually-minded man awakens. Ignorance must die for wisdom to be born. If a man is careless, negligent, and indolent in his work and suddenly begins to study and improve himself along all lines, the new, efficient, and industrious man is born, and the old careless, lazy, and confused man is dead.

In verse eighteen you are told that the spiritually-awakened man knows the only death, as the world looks at it, is the belief in death. *Death* is in us, not in the person in the coffin. *No man taketh it from you.* The absolute truth about it is this: When man is slain, he really slew himself even though another may have pulled the trigger loosing the bullet which killed him. The so-called murderer was simply an instrument fulfilling the slain man's state of consciousness. Consciousness is the only cause, and man himself is cause and effect. *No man cometh unto me, save I the Father draw him,* i.e., no manifestation or expression comes to me except my father (my dominant state of consciousness) attracts it. The inside or inner man is always causal, the outer is always effect. When we stand on the conviction that God is and that we dwell in the Secret Place of the Most High, no man can take anything away from us, no evil shall befall us, for we believe God is with us. This is faith. It is conviction.

In Japan last year (1955) a teacher told me about a Chinese woman during the Japanese raid who said to others, "Come under my umbrella; I believe in God." Bombs were falling all around her, but nothing touched her. The reason being that the place she stood was holy ground (her consciousness of God's Love and Presence). Living in the world, we should live in it in such a way that we refuse to hear or listen to anything which does not fill our soul with joy.

(28) *And I give unto them eternal life; and they shall never perish, neither shall any man pluck them out of my hand.*

This means that whatever consciousness touches or blesses, lasts forever. Once we taste God, or the Spirit of Truth, we are never the same again, and the

new understanding or comprehension is with us forever.

(33) *The Jews answered him, saying, For a good work
we stone thee not; but for blasphemy; and because that
thou, being a man, makest thyself God.*

The term *Jews* does not refer to a particular race of
people, but rather the average man or the man living
in the world-thought who thinks it is blasphemous
when he is told that man is God in expression walking the earth. He throws stones at those who proclaim
the truth in the sense he criticizes and condemns such
teachings as blasphemous because it is contrary to his
conditioning based on ignorant theories and beliefs
about God. The average man has a sort of worm of
the dust attitude.

(34) *Is it not written in your law, I said, Ye are gods?*

(38) *Though ye believe not me, believe the works:
that ye may know, and believe, that the Father is in me,
and I in him.*

In reality every man is a son of the Infinite and certainly the son possesses the same attributes, qualities,
and potencies of the Father. *Who, being in the form of
God, thought it not robbery to be equal with God.* PHIL.
2:6. Let us arise, awaken, and claim our divinity now.
Let us cease worshipping historical figures; rather let
us worship the One True God deep within us. The
Spirit within is God and when we align ourselves

with It, and call upon It *believing*, we will begin to do the works of Him who sent us. When we implicitly believe this, All Power at that moment is given to us in the heavens of our own mind. It is the Power and Action of God.

Chapter 11

(1) Now a certain man was sick, named Lazarus, of Bethany, the town of Mary and her sister Martha. (2) (It was that Mary which anointed the Lord with ointment, and wiped his feet with her hair, whose brother Lazarus was sick.) (3) Therefore his sisters sent unto him, saying, Lord, behold, he whom thou lovest is sick. (4) When Jesus heard that, he said, This sickness is not unto death, but for the glory of God, that the Son of God might be glorified thereby. (5) Now Jesus loved Martha, and her sister, and Lazarus. (6) When he had heard therefore that he was sick, he abode two days still in the same place where he was. (7) Then after that saith he to his disciples, Let us go into Judea again, (8) His disciples say unto him, Master, the Jews of late sought to stone thee; and goest thou thither again? (9) Jesus answered, Are there not twelve hours in the day? If any man walk in the day, he stumbleth not, because he seeth the light of this world. (10) But if a man walk in the night, he stumbleth, because there is no light in him.

Mary and Martha represent two states of consciousness, the outside and the inside, the material and spiritual. *Mary* refers to the inner or subjective side of life. *Martha* refers to the objective phase of life. Mary means also love of the spiritual values of life; Martha is the desire to minister to the physical needs of the sick and needy.

Lazarus is the brother (desire) of Martha and Mary (two aspects of consciousness, the conscious and subconscious mind). Lazarus represents the dead state within us. Our desire or ideal is dead because we have not made it alive or did not know that our consciousness could resurrect and make alive that which we claim and feel as true within. Lazarus is our dead, frozen, withered conception or desire which we have been trying to materialize for a long period of time. Man may have a disease; this is the dead state; health is not dead, but it is asleep in the man who is ill. Spiritual awareness represented by Jesus goes to awaken the dead state. The outer senses tell you that the body is diseased, but the spiritually awakened man proclaims, "I have been asleep to health. I am going to awaken out of this slumber and hypnotic spell of race belief."

The fifth verse means that love is a unity. Love is an emotional attachment. It is becoming absorbed in the reality of what you pray for, or mentally identifying and uniting with the thing desired. The steps of prayer are first, recognition of the Spiritual Power, second, acceptance of our desire, and third, the conviction in the reality of the unseen idea.

(14) *Then said Jesus unto them plainly, Lazarus is dead.* (16) *Then said Thomas, which is called Didymus, unto his fellow-disciples, Let us also go, that we may die with him.* (17) *Then when Jesus came, he found that he had lain in the grave four days already.*

Thomas is the doubter; it is an attitude of mind in all of us. This state of mind looks both ways and wonders if consciousness is the only power. Discouragement sets in and you say, "So be it." Here is a dialogue taking place between the lower self and the higher self in all of us, or between the three-dimensional self and the fourth-dimensional self, or the quarrel of our five senses with our spiritual knowledge or awareness. Notice when you pray how the senses try to dissuade you from believing that the Spiritual Power within you is the only Cause, and that it is Supreme and Sovereign. You must stand firm and know that with this One Power, all things are possible.

(23) *Jesus* (your illumined reason) *saith unto her, Thy brother shall rise again.* (24) *Martha saith unto him, I know that he shall rise again in the resurrection at the last day.*

Martha (our conscious, reasoning, argumentative mind) questions the possibility of resurrecting our desire, but the great truth is that our own I AM-NESS (consciousness) can resurrect and make visible that which we accept and feel as true within. Your own consciousness has the power to resurrect you from any state of limitation.

Verse twenty-four depicts Martha, the worldly-minded state of consciousness in all of us which looks into the far-distant future and says, "Some day I will reach my goal. Some day I will be happy." This is not the correct attitude, for we must realize that we can take our desire in consciousness now and bring it to birth immediately if only we will believe.

(38) *Jesus therefore again groaning in himself cometh to the grave. It was a cave, and a stone lay upon it.* (39) *Jesus said, Take ye away the stone.*

All of us may groan with the problem or difficulty, but we come to a definite decision in the mind that we can overcome and rise above it. The stone is the race belief, the fear, and acceptance of man-made laws. The health, joy, and peace we seek is held in the tomb by narrow, confining, restricted thoughts which imprison the life forces. The stone must be rolled away through faith. The man who wants the inner life of harmony, strength, and vitality to come forth must recognize and believe in the sovereignty of the Spiritual Power and his prayer of faith evokes the Presence of the Invisible and Omnipresent God. This is the Glory of God.

(40) *If thou wouldest believe, thou shouldest see the glory of God?*

The spiritual-minded man affirms the reality and completeness of the invisible idea regardless of external appearances. Elsewhere in the Bible you are told *an angel rolls away the stone. The angel* is a new attitude of mind, the feeling or conviction which precedes the demonstration.

(41) *Jesus lifted up his eyes, and said, Father, I thank thee that thou hast heard me.* (42) *And I knew that thou hearest me always.*

The latter verses give a magnificent formula for prayer. In praying for another you lift your concept of the other, seeing him radiant, happy, and free; then you give thanks for the accomplished fact.

For example, you pay the salesman in the department store for the fur coat, and you thank him for sending it. You have not yet received it, but you trust the concern and the man you are dealing with. There is no doubt in your mind that you will receive the coat you ordered. Likewise, when you turn to God in recognition, you are lifted up as you dwell on Him. You know that "He never faileth." You have an unshakeable confidence and trust in the Father of Lights in

Whom there is no variableness or shadow of turning. You know that He heareth you always because the nature of God is to turn to you as you turn to Him. The moment you move in thought and feeling to the Presence within and focus your attention on health and harmony for your friend, the Creative Power of God flows through your focal point of attention; this is God in action and It is Almighty.

The third step could be called recognition, acceptance, and the conviction that it is so. The quotation *Jesus cried with a loud voice*—means the sound of the answered prayer which is the voice or mood of authority. *Lazarus, come forth* represents the absolute faith in the working of the immutable, changeless law which always responds automatically to our inner knowing. It is the command from the inside of the one who knows, "I and my Father are one."

In verse forty-four we are told that *the face of the dead man was bound by a napkin*. If I meet you on the street, and your face is covered, I cannot recognize you. What we want is in our consciousness, and we cannot see consciousness. You cannot see faith and confidence in God. It is our invisible mind or mental atmosphere which, like saturated clouds, precipitate and fall as rain. Man hides and houses God. The Real Man is invisible; you do not see a mood, spirit, thought, feeling, faith, hopes, desires, ideals, and aspirations. Man himself is the napkin which hides the Invisible One.

I was naked and ye clothed me. MATT. 25:36. When man realizes that God is the very Life of him, the Living Spirit within, and when he turns to this Power in prayer, recognizing It, he has removed the napkin. He is then in the position to issue the command, "Loose him and let him go," which means unfettered life, freedom from all travails whereby man walks the earth a free, joyous being with the praise of God forever on his lips. He sees "tongues in trees, sermons in stones, songs in running brooks, and God in everything."

In verse fifty we recognize that it is expedient that one man should die. The *one who dies* is our desire. If it does not die in us, we remain frustrated. After the death of the belief in poverty comes health. Death of the belief in pain brings peace, and peace is the Power at the heart of God. "Peace be still."

Chapter 12

(1) Then Jesus six days before the passover came to Bethany, where Lazarus was which had been dead, whom he raised from the dead. (2) There they made him a supper; and Martha served: but Lazarus was one of them that sat at the table with him. (3) Then took Mary a pound of ointment of spikenard, very costly, and anointed the feet of Jesus, and wiped his feet with her hair: and the house was filled with the odour of the ointment. (4) Then saith one of his disciples, Judas Iscariot, Simon's son, which should betray him. (5) Why was not this ointment sold for three hundred pence, and given to the poor? (6) This he said, not that he cared for the poor: but because he was a thief, and had the bag, and bare what was put therein. (7) Then said Jesus, Let her alone: against the day of my burying hath she kept this. (8) For the poor always ye have with you: but me ye have not always. (9) Much people of the Jews therefore knew that he was there: and they came not for Jesus' sake only, but that they might see Lazarus also, whom he had raised from

the dead. (10) But the chief priests consulted that
they might put Lazarus also to death.

The *passover* means passing over, i.e., overcoming
problems or obstructions, being delivered from bondage. It represents freedom from the tyranny and confusion of the five senses. In the process of the passover,
we pass from one state of consciousness to another.

The Jews maintain an annual festival in commem-
oration of this escape from Egypt. *Egypt* means the
race mind which is full of belief in misery, pain, suffering, and unseen terrors. The greatest prison in the
world is the prison of the mind. ("Stone walls do not
a prison make, nor iron bars a cage."). We leave Egypt
and go to the true world of Mind and Spirit. This is
the Heaven of Jesus and the *house not made with hands*
eternal in the heavens as mentioned by Paul.

In the first verse it says Lazarus was present. This
means that the state of what we want is with us now
because our consciousness has lifted us up. *Spikenard*
infers faith. *Anointing the feet of Jesus* symbolizes our
entry into a delightful mood of love and expectancy.
Feet mean understanding, and *Jesus* means the Truth
or Spiritual awareness. *The ointment in Mary's hand*

represents the effusion and the pouring out of love from the sacred chalice of the heart, or the eternal verities, and the spiritual values of life. Nothing is too costly for the holy and blessed worship of God and His love.

Jesus in the Bible means our desire also, for the savior is always the fulfilled desire. The ideal state you wish must be anointed; i.e., felt as true before you can know the joy of the answered prayer. When the Bible says, "The house was filled with the odour of the ointment," it refers to the fact that we cannot suppress the joy which arises when our prayer is answered. We touch the Glory of the Lord within.

Wiping the feet of Jesus with her hair—the latter word means the Power of God. When the Omnipotence of God responds to our faith, our prayer is answered. We stand on the rock of faith and trust in the Omnipresence. We wipe, therefore, our feet with our hair, indicating our recognition of the supremacy and allegiance to the One Power, and we know no other. We know God, we dwell with Him, and rest under the Shadow of the Almighty. *None shall stay its hand and say unto it, what doest thou?*

In verse six we read *Judas was a thief and had the bag.* Here is a story of salvation, or the solution to any problem. All stories in the Bible are for the purpose of teaching us how to get out of trouble and realize our freedom. *Judas* means our problem or state of limitation. *Money*, or the bag which he carried, symbolizes our need or lack. The *poor which are always with us* are our sense of lack in regard to wisdom, truth, and knowledge of God. Many people are poor in joy, laughter, good will, and though they may have millions of dollars, yet they may be very poor in the understanding of God and His laws. Your poor state now is your problem. This poor state is good in the sense that it is an incentive to you, urging you to rise up and conquer. You have the power to do so; thereby you discover your Divinity and your Inherent Powers.

Through your problem you grow, expand, and unfold. Look for the little chink of light in your present darkness or difficulty and you will find it. One of the ancient meanings of the word *crisis* is opportunity. Now is your opportunity to call forth the Wisdom and Power of God which will solve your problem, heal your body, and dissolve the clouds of despair. Many think when they have lost money, they have lost everything. They forget that when they lose peace of mind or love, they have lost the only real things in the world. Men, in their state of sleep and mass hypnosis by the world-mind or race-consciousness, expect to lose health, harmony, and the abundance of God's riches. Ask some of your fellow-students in the path of life if they caught the flu this year. They will reply, "No, not yet," indicating that they expect it sooner or later.

The *Judas* in us always carries the bag, our sense of need. We must give up the sense of need before we can understand salvation or the solution to our problems. Judas betrays. *To betray* is to reveal. Your problem (Judas) reveals your savior (your desire). Every difficulty, problem, and limitation has its solution in the form of a desire. The realization of the desire is always our savior. Your problem, or Judas, is saying to you now, "Stand aside and let the subjective wisdom anoint your intellect, revealing to you the way you should go or the decision you should make." If you were possessed of a higher wisdom you would not have the problem.

The electrician solves the problem of a short circuit in your home because of his higher knowledge or wisdom regarding the laws of electricity. Let us suppose you are not possessed with this wisdom regarding the principle of electricity; then to you it is a problem. Look at your Judas now and rejoice; it is your marvelous opportunity to prove the Power of God in you. Judas is reported to have said, "Why was not this ointment sold for three hundred pence, and given to the poor?" Never give attention to the limited, morbid state. Never indulge in a negative emotion. When we give our attention to the squalid, the mean, and the low, that is what we create in our lives. Likewise to fight and resist the problem is to magnify it. Feel a sense of oneness with your ideal state which is your Jesus. Desire without fear is manifestation.

(12) *Much people that were come to the feast, when they heard that Jesus was coming to Jerusalem, (13) Took branches of palm trees, and went forth to meet him, and cried, Hosanna: Blessed is the King of Israel that cometh in the name of the Lord. (14) And Jesus, when he had found a young ass, sat thereon; as it is written, (15) Fear not, daughter of Sion: behold, thy King cometh, sitting on an ass's colt.*

Here we have the Palm Sunday story. *Palms* are symbolic of triumph, victory, and achievement. Jesus is depicted as riding on a young colt. *The colt* symbolizes our new, unbridled ideal or desire which is not yet disciplined or appropriated. *Jesus riding the animal* means that we must live with the animated state of consciousness or mood and sustain it until we enter Jerusalem, which means the city of peace. In other words, we live in the mental atmosphere of acceptance until it jells within us and we are at peace about it in our own mind. When there is no longer any quarrel in our conscious or subconscious mind, our prayer is answered. The spirit within validates and brings to pass all such mental agreements. We receive only what we have accepted in consciousness.

To ride the colt is to ride the mood. It means perseverance. The trainer of a horse is firm but kind. He lets the horse know who is master. Your dominant mental attitude is the master; it determines where you shall go. Then we cry, "Hosanna!" which is peace or the Divine solution. *Blessed is the King of Israel that cometh in the name of the Lord. He who cometh* is our desire. The *name* (nature) of the Lord (law) is to express that which is impressed. To be blessed is to realize our desire.

(23) *And Jesus answered them, saying, The hour is to come, that the Son of man should be glorified. (24) Verily, verily, I say unto you, Except a corn of wheat fall into the ground and die, it abideth alone: but if it die, it bringeth forth much fruit.*

Death is always a change of form. When we get new ideas, we change our thought. This change is the death of our old way of thinking, and we come out of the rut of lack and limitation. *The corn of wheat that dies in the soil* (our consciousness) is our ideal or desire. As long as we have the desire, we are frustrated and unhappy. There is a war in the mind. When we identify mentally and emotionally with our desire, it dies and passes into the subjective realm of feeling; we are at peace about it. After a little while it appears on the screen of space. Then the new heaven and new earth spoken of in The Book of Revelation come to pass.

The new heaven is your new state of consciousness which automatically recreates your world to correspond with your new mental world. The old man and his old fashioned ideas and concepts must die before the new man can be resurrected.

Let us now look at the key verses in the rest of the chapter omitting as much as possible all the repetitious verses of the Bible which tend to duplicate what we have already written.

He that loveth his life shall lose it; and he that hateth his life in this world shall keep it unto life eternal. 12:25.

Many people grossly misinterpret this wonderful passage by renouncing and giving up the comforts and pleasures of life. Self-effacement, abuse of the body, the belief in poverty, and flagellation of the body in order to serve the truth, are superstitious, immature ideas which deny the divine birthright of man. Man is here to express God in all His Glory and Abundance. What we should lose is our false concept of God and our low estimate of ourselves and claim a real oneness with God. If we love (emotional attachment) limitation, we join with it and are one with it; then we multiply negative conditions in our lives; we constantly find ourselves manifesting greater limitation until finally everything is taken away from us. We have lost our lives in the sense that we possess no zest in living. We are dead to joy, love, and beauty.

He that hateth his life in this world shall keep it. One of the meanings of *hate* in the Bible is to reject, to put away, to refuse. We hate our former life when we reject negative imagery and suggestions of any nature whatsoever. The dope addict hates his life when he transforms himself mentally and becomes a new man. His habitual thinking made him a dope fiend. When he learns of the tremendous dynamo within himself, called sometimes the subconscious mind and begins to use it, he works wonders in his life. He now runs a new motion picture of himself in his imagination, the constructive, directed use of which is called the workshop of God. The subconscious mind faithfully reproduces the exact image and likeness of his mental pattern. We must never forget that our habitual thinking shapes and molds our destiny; it makes us what we are today. Having changed his mental attitude, man is manifesting life eternal. This means the enjoyment of peace, harmony, and prosperity, not only on this plane, but down through the corridors of time, through the pathways of eternity until time, as we know it, shall be no more. No man can look upon the face of God (the truth) and live the old life.

Let us look upon God's handiwork. If we look aright, we will become conscious of the abundant life. We will see God in the laughter of the child, in the kiss of a loved one, and in the smile of a friend.

And I, if I be lifted up from the earth, will draw all men unto me. This he said, signifying what death he should die. 12:32–33.

It is obvious to those who have eyes to see and ears to hear that this is not a reference to a physical death. It is purely psychological, written in figurative, oriental language telling all of us how to rise to higher levels of awareness. In the prayer-process you must lift your concepts up to the point of acceptance, then the manifestation will follow. Your physical senses report their findings which at best are depressing. In prayer you go within to the inner realm of spiritual truths, anchoring your mind there; thereby being fed with faith, courage, strength, and power which transcend the ordinary physical senses. You are then lifted up, the old state dies, and the new state of consciousness is resurrected; this is a psychological death. You correct what you see in the world of appearances by what you know about God and His Omnipresence. We can never manifest our good in a depressed state. We must go up the mountain (high state of consciousness) and thrill to the new state. Unless we behold our vision and ascend by contemplating its reality, we cannot gain the new perspective by which we may dissipate the fearsome shadows seen when we are in the valley.

Walk while ye have the light. 12:35.

The *light* refers to Divine Intelligence, the God within which leads and guides us as we call upon it. We must go forth knowing that we are Divinely led in all our ways; then only right action and expression will prevail. If we are in confusion, we walk in the darkness and know not whither we go.

In verse forty we are told that people's eyes are blinded in the sense they refuse to see the truth about themselves. They reject anything new and remain blind to their Inner Powers. Their heart is hardened because they still adhere to their old grudges and resentments. They are identified with negative emotions, full of creedal prejudices, etc. If they would open their eyes and ears and hear the truth about themselves, they would be healed and at peace.

He that rejecteth me, and receiveth not my word, hath one that judgeth him: the word that I have spoken, the same shall judge him in the last day. 12:48.

The one that judgeth is our own mind, for all judgment is given to the son. Dr. Nicoll points out the son means your mind. It means also your thought. By your thought you are judging all day long.

Our mental state judges us and rebuilds us according to our faith or conviction. There is no one to accuse or punish us except ourselves. Man gives himself everything; actually all he is, has, or experiences is pressed out of his own consciousness. We judge ourselves by our conviction of ourselves or others. How do we judge the other? Do we see a sick person or a well one? If you see a person ill, and say to yourself, "I hope he will be better," you are judging wrongly. But if you treat him scientifically, realizing he is healed, made whole and perfect, you are judging righteously.

By our words we are justified and by our words we are condemned. Our word is a movement of consciousness and the automatic execution of the law which never varies. Let us judge all men righteously by seeing them as they ought to be—happy, radiant, and perfect.

Chapter 13

(1) Now before the feast of the passover, when Jesus knew that his hour was come that he should depart out of this world unto the Father, having loved his own which were in the world, he loved them unto the end. (2) And supper being ended, the devil having put into the heart of Judas Iscariot, Simon's son, to betray him; (3) Jesus knowing that the Father had given all things into his hands, and that he was come from God, and went to God; (4) He riseth from supper, and laid aside his garments; and took a towel, and girded himself. (5) After that he poureth water into a bason, and began to wash the disciples' feet, and to wipe them with the towel wherewith he was girded. (6) Then cometh he to Simon Peter: and Peter saith unto him, Lord, dost thou wash my feet? Jesus answered and said unto him, What I do thou knowest not now; but thou shalt know hereafter. (8) Peter saith unto him, Thou shalt never wash my feet. Jesus answered him, If I wash thee not, thou hast no part with me. (9) Simon Peter saith unto him, Lord, not my feet only, but

also my hands and my head. (10) Jesus saith to
him, He that is washed needeth not save to wash
his feet, but is clean every whit: and ye are clean,
but not all.

The feast of the passover is something that is going on all the time in the mind of the praying individual. Passover is, of course, celebrated by the Jews and is a very wonderful and inspiring religious drama and festival. The outer ceremony and celebration is intended to commemorate the deliverance of the children of Israel from the bondage and tyranny of Pharaoh. There is the mystical and psychological passover in which all of us are interested; as a matter of fact, the only purpose of the Biblical stories is to bring about a psychological change, an inner transformation.

As you read the Bible, you realize that the man, Jesus, was known to everyone; moreover there was no occasion to procure lanterns to search for him. All the people knew where he was. You must, therefore, look for the hidden or inner meaning. The drama says that he told his disciples he was going to die and that one of them would betray him. Wouldn't you get rid of a man in your organization who was about to betray all your business plans and secrets? If you were doing some scientific research work for the United States Government and you knew that there was a spy working, stealing all the government's secrets, would you retain him in your employment, or wouldn't you see to it that he was discharged or otherwise displaced at once? I am sure you would. You will receive an answer to these questions as you follow the explanation given in this and succeeding chapters.

In the prayer-process you pass over from the state of lack to the feeling of fulfillment. If fearful, you pass over into the mood of confidence and faith in the same manner as a soldier wrote about in the Korean War. When there seemed to be no way out, his knees were knocking, and he was white with fear, he kept repeating out loud, "God is with me; I have no fear." A great sense of calm and peace came over him; he was not hurt or wounded, and succeeded in escaping from the trap of certain death. He experienced the passover; i.e., the psychological change which comes over man as he humbly, devotedly turns to the Spiritual Presence for his deliverance and release. To experience the passover you must become identified with the ideal you hope to achieve, remaining faithful and loyal to this ideal. You succeed in crucifying it by your faithfulness; you will also resurrect it without the aid of anyone.

In verse two where it says *and supper being ended* symbolizes the end of the psychological feast. *Judas Iscariot* signifies limitation of any kind. *Iscariot* means of many cities which refers to many states of consciousness. It is said he is Simon's son. *Simon* means to hear. In other words, if you are hearing bad news or indulging in a sense of limitation, it means negative, subjective hearing. *To betray* means to reveal. Your problem always reveals your savior or solution in the form of your desire. A solution is always the opposite of a problem.

In verse three it says that *Jesus was come from God* and means that God responds to us through our desire. When you mentally accept your good or desire, it may be said in Biblical language that you *went to God. Jesus laying aside his garments* refers to the revealing of the process of creation in phallic symbology. *To take a towel and gird yourself* is to assume a new attitude of mind, knowing that your own consciousness is the creative power, rejecting completely any other power.

After that he poureth water into a bason, and began to wash the disciples' feet, and to wipe them with the towel wherewith he was girded. 13:5. This is what we really do in the prayer-process or passing over from our limitation to freedom. *The basin* is your mind where you pour all your thoughts, concepts, feelings, and beliefs. *The water* represents the truth which now flows into your mind that God is the only Presence and the only Power. You announce the truth to your assembled faculties (disciples); you rehearse all that you know about the Creative Process and boldly and firmly assert that as you give your attention and devotion to your desire, the God-Power within will honor your claim. You insist that your inner feeling or awareness must and will be made manifest. You remain steadfast and loyal to the inner causal principle. All your thoughts, concepts, and mental pictures are now bathed in the light of faith, trust, and confidence in the Power or Cause. *You are washing your disciples'* (mental attitudes) *feet* and wiping them clean of all fear, doubt, and anxieties based on belief in other powers and causes. You have come to the place where you have a sense of wholeness or oneness with your good. You are girded by the towel of an inner certitude, a conviction that your prayer is already answered in Divine Mind and all is well.

Feet represent understanding. Your feet are washed when you know that any idea felt as true is objectified. Our faith in God is real and firm when we are incapable of hearing anything other than that which fills our soul with joy and gladness. It is then that *Peter's feet are washed. Peter* means faith in God. Peter is a faculty of mind in all of us. You can discipline yourself to the point that no matter what the five senses reveal, or what conditions may suggest, you remain unmoved, unperturbed because your inner hearing is, "He never faileth." This is why the scripture says that, "He that is washed needeth not save to wash his feet."

The *secret parts of man* are revealed when he removes the towel symbolically pointing out that the creative power is our own awareness, our own mind, and consciousness. Man is also the towel as he is covering God. God indwells him and he is the house of God. Man's false beliefs have clothed him in rags and sickness. When you meditate on the singleness of the Creative Power, you will begin to reveal strength, power, wisdom, and radiant health. You are taking off the outer coverings (false beliefs and negative attitudes) and revealing the spiritual sovereignty of the eternal verities and Godlike ideals.

In verse seven reference is made to faith. We must reach forward and mentally grasp the ideal we seek even though we may not know how the answer will come. *Faith is the substance of things hoped for, the evidence of things not seen.* Heb. 11:1. When our concept gives us the thrill of being or having what we want, this is the evidence of things not seen.

There is much repetition in the remaining verses of this chapter. We will, therefore, take the key verses and the inner meaning thereof.

If I then, your Lord and Master, have washed your feet; ye also ought to wash one another's feet. 13:14.

Your Lord, as you read this, is really your spiritual awareness, your dominant feeling about God's Truths. Who is in control of your mind, your emotions, and reactions? Is it Wisdom? If your thoughts are wise, your actions will be wise. *Your feet are washed;* i.e., when you are possessed of a new understanding that thoughts are things, that as you think and act toward others, so they shall act toward you. You will wash all men by wishing for them all the treasures of Infinity. To understand all is to forgive all. You wash the minds of all by seeing God in all. Keep on washing your disciples' feet. Be humble and sincere. Free your mind of arrogance, spiritual pride, the holier than thou attitude, and other destructive attitudes.

To be humble does not mean to be a doormat; it means giving all power and allegiance to the God within. You can refuse to go along mentally with self-justification, the feeling of hurt, others owe you an apology, that you were treated unfairly, etc. Let the God in you salute the God in all. Every time you pray it requires a washing and scrubbing of your disciples' feet (your faculties and mental attitudes). If you pray for a healing and you have a sense of guilt, envy, jealously, or ill will, remember that your entire mentality enters into the prayer-process.

If, for example, you have unresolved conflicts or deep-seated grudges, the Life-Process will flow through this contaminated state depriving you in a large measure of the good you seek. When the pipe in the kitchen sink is blocked with debris or rust, the water may not come out at all, or if it does, it comes forth sparingly and contaminated with the foreign materials. The water was waiting to come forth all the time, but the pipeline was at fault. Sever yourself from all negative emotions. Clothe yourself with the garments of love, beauty, and good will to all. Chop the heads off of envy, pretense, jealousy, and recriminations of all kinds, and consume them with the fire of Divine Love for all.

Now I tell you before it come, that, when it is come to pass, ye may believe that I am he. 13:19.

You are always predicting what is to come when you pray. You can have a preview of that which is to come by imagining the end in your mind, rejoicing and thrilling in that mental picture until it is completely absorbed in your mentality. When you experience it on the objective plane, you receive that which you first saw in your mind. You had predicted what was to come to pass through your faith and belief. *Ye may believe that I am he.* You are what you contemplate and feel as true; therefore you have discovered that your I Am is your savior.

*He it is, to whom I shall give a sop, when I have
dipped it. And when he had dipped the sop, he gave it
to Judas Iscariot, the son of Simon. 13:26. And after the
sop Satan entered into him. Then said Jesus unto him,
That thou doest, do quickly. 13:27.*

Judas, in *The Dictionary of the Sacred Language,*
is a symbol of limitation, your problem, or difficulty.
The limited state is necessary for our unfoldment.
This drama of the crucifixion is psychological from
beginning to end. Our problem (Judas) is our opportunity to discover the God within; this is why Judas
(our sense of lack, fear, sickness, etc.) betrays or
reveals the desire, the acceptance of which is the savior which sets us free. In other words, to put it in the
simplest language, our Judas reveals our Jesus. Jesus is
that which saves. What saves you now if you are sick?
Health would save you. Your inner realization of the
Infinite Healing Presence saturating your whole being
would free you now, this minute, as you read and apply
that simple truth.

Sop represents food, i.e., spiritual food, or knowledge of the Inner Power. When we read of Jesus giving
food to Judas out of the dish, it means that you are
feeding on the knowledge there is only One Power;
then the foolish, weird ideas of a suffering savior,
an avenging god, plus your fears are no longer tena-
ble. You are feasting on the Invisible Power you have

discovered within. Your own thought kindles the response of the Almighty Spirit within. You now know and are fully aware that you are endowed with Power from On High which lies in the depths of your own subconscious, and you can create your own condition.

In discovering your Hidden Powers all your former fears, tensions, and anxieties collapse and are burnt up. You have recharged and revivified yourself mentally by instilling into your household the mood of confidence, faith, and trust. You have found your Jesus and you no longer look for personal saviors either in the past, the present, or the future. You discover you are your own savior. It is then that your Jesus, or your spiritual awareness and knowledge, has fed your mind so that the limitation or problem falls away and dies of neglect, and you resurrect your desire.

Judas (you with your problems) was considered poor (lack of knowledge of God), but now you are rich because you have feasted on God's Eternal Love, Peace, Joy, and Perfection here and now. Whatever your problem is as you read these pages, you can solve it by meditating on the solution or answer to the point of conviction; then the Judas (limited) state is changed to the Jesus or saving state of consciousness which saves you.

In the days when the scripture was written and in parts of the world today *breaking bread with another* is a sacred ceremony. Psychologically this story represents a spiritual feast. *Dipping the sop* means you have become so enthusiastic and absorbed that you have actually impregnated your mind to the point of conviction regarding the truths you affirmed.

That thou doest, do quickly. Don't fool around. Be quick to realize the truth and galvanize yourself into the feeling of being what you long to be. It is said Judas hanged himself. We hang ourselves by our own hand; i.e., we die to the old and we live in the new by realization of the truth. The old man must die before the new man is born.

What happened to the sick man who is now healed? He hanged the former man, and the new man in God (in perfect health) is born. A man changes when he gets a new viewpoint, a new set of values. When you have a spiritual standard by which you judge all thoughts, ideas, and concepts, you are a new man.

If, for example, you mentally dwell in the consciousness or awareness of God's endless, tireless, unfailing supply and that He giveth the increase, you will magnify and expand along all lines. If you do not know the laws of mind, you are Judas thinking in terms of lack, limitation, chaos, etc; thereby bringing more limitation into your life. Develop the Jesus Christ Consciousness now by scientifically directing your thinking and mental imagery to conform with the pattern on the mount and you will expand and unfold in a wonderful way both within and without.

Wilt thou lay down thy life for my sake? Verily, verily, I say unto thee, The cock shall not crow, till thou hast denied me thrice. 13:38.

Peter must deny Jesus three times. You must have no master or lord but God—The One Power. We must categorically and emphatically mentally reject all other powers but the One Primal Cause, the Spirit within. The numeral three means conviction. If we have a master, we are slaves. This is why He says, "Call no man master." Man is not a serf. He has been given dominion.

The cock crows in the morning to herald the dawn. The cock also crows after the creative act. All this is used in the Bible as a symbol to remind man that he will utter the cry of victory and triumph over all problems when he is acquainted with the Creative Power within him. When we are convinced beyond a shadow of a doubt that our own I AM-NESS is our Lord and Master, we know no other. We know whatever we attach feelingly to I AM we become; then the cock crows in us because this truth is a new day in our life. It is a symbol and the awakening to God.

Reject the world and its false beliefs; become alive to God; then you are Peter denying all earthly masters. You have done it three times because it is now a conviction in your heart and you say, "It is finished!"

Chapter 14

(1) Let not your heart be troubled: ye believe in God, believe also in me. (2) In my Father's house are many mansions: if it were not so, I would have told you. I go to prepare a place for you. (3) And if I go and prepare a place for you, I will come again, and receive you unto myself; that where I am, there ye may be also. (4) And whither I go ye know, and the way ye know. (5) Thomas saith unto him, Lord, we know not whither thou goest; and how can we know the way? (6) Jesus saith unto him, I am the way, the truth, and the life: no man cometh unto the Father, but by me. (7) If ye had known me, ye should have known my Father also: and from henceforth ye know him, and have seen him. (8) Philip saith unto him, Lord shew us the Father, and it sufficeth us. (9) Jesus saith unto him, Have I been so long time with you, and yet hast thou not known me, Philip? he that hath seen me hath seen the Father; and how sayest thou then, Shew us the Father? (10) Believest thou not that I am in the Father, and the Father in me? the words that I speak unto you I speak

not of myself: but the Father that dwelleth in me,
he doeth the works. (11) Believe me that I am in
the Father, and the Father in me: or else believe
me for the very works' sake. (12) Verily, verily, I
say unto you, He that believeth on me, the works
that I do shall he do also; and greater works than
these shall he do; because I go unto my Father.
(13) And whatsoever ye shall ask in my name,
that will I do, that the Father may be glorified in
the Son. (14) If ye shall ask any thing in my name,
I will do it.

The *many mansions in our Father's house* refer to many states of consciousness. We are always living in states of mind. For example, as you read this chapter, you realize you are living with your dreams, yearnings, urges, aspirations, thoughts, feelings, imaginings, vacuities, and emotions. All these are very real. You meet a man in the morning, he seems happy and joyous. In the afternoon the same man may be petulant, crotchety, cantankerous, and irascible. In the evening he may be pious, benign, and serene. He is living in many mansions during the day. It is quite true that a man may be living in a palace physically and at the same time be living in a mental prison of fear, apprehension, and ill will. The real prison is the prison of the mind. If a man is bedridden, of what good is it to be living in a palace? If a man goes to work in the morning with a song in his heart, he is living in a wonderful mansion of the mind.

God is Infinite; therefore man is infinite. Never in eternity could man exhaust the glory and beauty within him. Man is capable of an infinite number of conceptions of himself. We are actually living in the infinite dimension of mind at this time because we know that the Fathomless Being is within us, and there is no end to our unfoldment or expansion.

I go to prepare a place for you. If we want to leave our present mansion (state of limitation), we must rise in consciousness and become one with our ideal. When we fix this state to the point of conviction, we have succeeded in preparing the place which we will ultimately occupy. We must, in other words, build into our mentality the mental equivalent of what we desire; then we have arrived at the point of acceptance in our mind which is followed by the outer manifestation.

Verse six does not refer to a man. It means man's inner consciousness is the way to health, freedom, and peace of mind. Your I AM-NESS is the door to all manifestations and expressions. You become what you contemplate. Your consciousness or awareness is the truth because whatever you feel as true will come to pass. The realization of your desire would free you this moment if you were sick or in prison. This would be the truth that would set you free.

You can make a test for yourself. Begin to believe that life is harmonious and friendly and people are wonderful. You will find life will take on a new meaning because of your new attitude. It is done unto you as you believe. You are operating a law of your own mind. You have discovered a truth which sets you free from despondency, gloom, and loneliness. When you believe the world is good, you discover life corresponds to your attitude and your world becomes good. To know that your thoughts and feelings direct your destiny enables you to soar aloft above the problems of the world and dwell on the solution in the realm of spirit and mind. You know that wherever your consciousness is, there will your body be also. Your feet and hands will go where your consciousness is. If you say, "I am poor," and feel the poverty state, your consciousness attracts poverty so the poor get poorer and the rich get richer.

No man cometh unto the Father, but by me. This means that no manifestation comes to us save our own consciousness draws it. The *me* referred to is our own I AM-NESS. Your I AM-NESS is the mother and father of all ideas. When Philip says, "Show us the Father," he is calling forth our dominant mood. One cannot see a mood or a feeling. When you actually become aware of the principle of inner causation, you have discovered your God or your Father in Heaven. Having now discovered the Principle of Life, you must begin to use it wisely. Never permit the suggestion of defeat and impotency to inhibit the free flow of this inner life. Whatever you become aware of determines whether you see lack or confusion or whether you see opulence, order, and harmony in your world.

We cannot see a principle but we can see its effects. *Philip* is a trainer of horses, which indicates a quality of persistence. You are calling forth the quality of mind termed Philip when you positively refuse to let the images presented by your five senses dampen or becloud your enthusiasm and determination to reach your goal. You know you must go where your vision is.

He that hath seen me hath seen the Father. In other words, your own consciousness is the Father of everything made manifest in your world. All your experiences, circumstances, and conditions are represented as the *son* bearing witness to the Father, the state of consciousness which is the cause behind your present world. Through your new awareness of this Infinite Power within, look away beyond present conditions and facts, focus your attention on your announced goal, claim boldly that God's peace, love, joy, and happiness are yours now. When you find conditions in the external world tend to frighten or dismay you, turn immediately to the Divine Presense within and announce your good here and now. Let nothing put a damper on your uplifted spirit. Even though your good cannot be discerned with the naked eye, your Inner Light becomes a lamp unto your feet and you find yourself walking on the pathway of His Light. When beset with worries, trials, or tribulations of any kind, you place all your trust in God knowing like Job of old that His candle shines upon your head and by His Light you walk through darkness.

He that hath seen me (desire made manifest) *hath seen the Father,* which is the inner mood or conviction. This refers to an inner seeing and an inner knowing. In verse twelve you are told that the *works which Jesus did any man can do and even greater things.* First of all we must realize our oneness with God and know that we are immersed in this Infinite Godhead—one with the Whole. What the Bible is really saying is that the Power which Jesus used, any man who walks the earth can use. The same Healing Presence is available to all. The same Wisdom and Intelligence may be used by all. We must become alert, alive, and awaken to our tremendous potentialities to the degree that we believe we are sons of God and one with Omnipotence, to that degree do we manifest His Power and Glory.

Jesus was a man born in the same way that all other men are born, but he attained unparalleled heights through discipline, meditation, prayer, and communion with God. There is really no reason why any man could not excel Jesus in wisdom and power for, after all, there is no limit to the Glory and Wisdom which is man. God is Infinite, hence man is infinite also. It would be silly to say that Jesus had reached the ultimate—there is no end. He, together with Moses, Elias, Buddha, and many others are undoubtedly living in some fabulous dimension of mind revealing more and more of the glories of HE WHO IS.

If ye shall ask any thing in my name, I will do it— we ask in the *name* when we appropriate the nature of our desire. We must assume the naturalness of the thing we ask. We must wear the garment (psychological attitude) until it becomes an embodiment. To continue in the mood or feeling of mental possession is to make manifest your desire. Potentialities of all states are within man.

We will now take the key verses of the balance of this most interesting chapter giving the meat or pure essence of its contents.

And I will pray the Father, and he shall give you
another Comforter, that he may abide with you for ever.
14:16

The Mystical Power is always our Comforter and
Redeemer. While writing this chapter, I was inter-
rupted by a long distance telephone call from an old
friend. His voice was strident and angry saying, "My
enemies are out to ruin and undermine me and my
business." Obviously he did not know that the Comforter was within and abides with him forever. He
discovered his savior within by following a simple,
spiritual technique. He began praying in this fashion,
"These two men (his so-called enemies) are reflecting
more and more of God and His goodness every day.
They have the same hopes, desires, and aspirations
as I have. They want peace, harmony, love, joy, and
abundance, and so do I. I wish for them all of God's
blessings. Our relationship is harmonious, peaceful,
and full of Divine understanding. They wish to do
the right thing according to the Golden Rule as I do.
I salute the God in them now. I see them as God sees
them—whole, pure, and perfect. It is wonderful."

This was the essence of the prayer I gave him over
the telephone. I told him to let the impression and
feeling of these thoughts sink into his deeper mind
until he was possessed by their truth. Furthermore, I
related to him as he continued to bless in the above

way, there would be a great sense of inner release, like a cleansing of the soul. I let him know he would feel at peace, and the Comforter would come like a river of peace flooding his mind and heart. He practiced the above technique in a whole-souled, devotional manner and discovered that he actually secreted this mystical, healing Power from the depths of himself which brought about a perfect, harmonious solution in the realm of his relationship to the men in question. A magnificent change had taken place between them. He discovered his Comforter and Counselor to be the God within us all.

Another simple method of explaining the meaning of the Comforter is to look upon your Jesus as your ideal or desire. It is obvious your desire must pass away before the Comforter comes. When you possess your desire in consciousness, you no longer desire it. You do not seek that which you have, but you must first have it in consciousness. If your desire is always ahead of you, if it is always in the future, you never get it. The reason for this is that if our consciousness is in a state of futurity, we are not in the present, and all prayers function in the present tense. We accept the is-ness of our desire now by seeing the accomplished fact in perfect confidence, peace, and poise. We must never be worried, hurried, anxious, or looking for results. We must simply know that it is so.

Even the Spirit of truth; whom the world cannot receive, because it seeth him not, neither knoweth him: but ye know him; for he dwelleth with you, and shall be in you. 14:17.

The Comforter is also called the Holy Spirit or the feeling of wholeness or oneness with our ideal. Our external world will always reject this Spirit of Truth as long as we live in moods of fear, doubt, and anxiety. The Comforter is a synonym for God. The Universal is in the individual, and the individual is in the Universal. To know the Truth is to know the Comforter; this is your freedom. God is all there is. God is no respecter of persons. The law in and of itself has no morals. The rain falls on the good and the evil.

Recently I was engaged by a firm of attorneys to pray for a solution. They had a long, drawn-out case and their client was, as they said, completely disgusted. One of the attorneys spent an hour with me twice weekly. This lawyer understood that what he wanted was a divine, harmonious solution. Furthermore, he knew he would experience the reaction of his dominant, mental attitude. His thoughts did not dwell on taking away anything from the opposing side or depriving them of their rights. He knew he would experience the result of the negative use of such a law. He claimed Divine right action and right decision which would bless all. The law of his mind accepted his aim and desire embodying and bringing it to pass. His aim and his motive were good. The law is amoral. Our morality is concerned with the way we use it.

Let us take a lawsuit. If one party is lying and has the motive or intension to cheat another or defraud him in some way, he is misusing the law because it will respond to him according to his thoughts and motives. His motive is his inner feeling of guilt and sense of wrong doing; therefore, he must experience the automatic response of the law which is the reaction to his thoughts and feelings. My attitude in legal matters is not to take sides, but to know that God cannot really sue God, therefore the law of harmony and Divine justice prevails, and adhering to that regardless of appearances or judgment to the contrary, God is never late. Hold fast to that which is good and right, never desiring in any way whatsoever to harm or deprive another of his good.

He that loveth me not keepeth not my sayings: and the word which ye hear is not mine, but the Father's which sent me. 14:24.

The words that I speak unto you, they are spirit, and they are life. 6:63.

Words represent your thoughts and feelings. A *word* in the Bible means your conviction, your inner feeling, or awareness. You send your word to heal another when you are absolutely convinced of the presence of wholeness and perfection in the other. Your word is your unshakeable conviction that what you have claimed as true is true in your heart. Your word is then God's word, meaning it is a state of consciousness which manifests itself. In the language of the Bible your words are spirit and they are life.

But the Comforter, which is the Holy Ghost, whom the Father will send in my name, he shall teach you all things, and bring all things to your remembrance, whatsoever I have said unto you. 14:26.

The Holy Ghost means the feeling of wholeness or oneness. Whole means one piece or the mental state of at-one-ment with your good. Your mind is no longer divided, you have realized your desire, and you are therefore at peace. The Holy Ghost refers to your inner feeling of wholeness or answered prayer. The word *Ghost*, means breath, life, or feeling. The deduction is simple when the feeling of inner certainty comes, that is the visit of the Holy Ghost.

Love is the fulfilling of the law. When you are filled full of the feeling of being what you long to be, you have fulfilled the law. You have wished for everyone all the good things of life. You are full of love and good will to all. You have used the law righteously to bless yourself, granting the same blessing to all. You are at peace with yourself and the whole world. You have found the Comforter, the spirit of peace and good will, which come when we pour out love on all people everywhere, clothing them with the garment of salvation and the robe of righteousness.

In verse twenty-eight where it says, "*I go away, and come again unto you,*" our ideal, our Jesus (desire) goes into consciousness. Whatever we feel as true within, we will experience on the without. Our ideal must go away in order to manifest or be objectified. First must come the impression in the mind; then the expression, referred to as going away and coming back. It is so very simple, you wonder why people make such a mystery of it all.

My father is greater than I. 14:28. This means that the creator is always greater than his creation.

The thinker is greater than his thoughts. The artist is greater than his art. Our consciousness is greater than its conception. Knowing this, we realize we have the power to transcend our present concept of ourselves for there is no end to our unfoldment.

And now I have told you before it came to pass, that, when it is come to pass, ye might believe. 14:29.

The writer has seen many events before they happened in this three dimensional plane. I am sure you have witnessed events which transpired later. Perhaps you saw events in a dream, like J. W. Dunne, the great mathematician, before they happened here on this plane. You can consciously construct the realization of your wish in your mind now, today. Sit still, experience in your imagination the desirable result, see the end, and rejoice in the finished or accomplished fact, such as the sale of your home and the success of a loved one. You have seen it before it came to pass. You can definitely predict the outcome. You have had a preview of things to come. What you have seen, heard, and felt in your imagination, the theatre of your mind, must be experienced on the screen of space.

Hereafter I will not talk much with you: for the prince of this world cometh, and hath nothing in me. 14:30.

This verse signifies that when fear-thoughts come to your mind, there is no response from you, for you are at peace, and your mind is disciplined to hear the good only. You are no longer a victim of the collective race suggestions. We must become like Daniel in the lions' den who looked to the Only Light for his solution and salvation. All the expressions in our world have no life apart from the ideas behind them. The idea is substantial and permanent. The form is the expression or the idea clothed. The perceiver and the thing perceived are one. We look at a mountain and all of us see a mountain, indicating one mind common to all men. We could not see a mountain except the idea was conceived in our consciousness. If we see something in the external world that displeases us, we have permitted it to disturb us. We must change our relationship to it; then it will not affect us. If a man reads the morning news and permits it to disturb him, that is a bad mood. He has let the prince of this world come in and agitate him.

Arise, let us go hence. 14:31. This verse means to rise up in consciousness and go within to the Secret Place. It is what the disciples meant when they said to the beggar at the gate, *Silver and gold have I none; but such as I have give I thee, Rise up and walk.* ACTS 3:6. Giving a man money does not heal him of the consciousness of lack. Give him wisdom, the pearl of great price; teach him the know how; then he will never beg again. When he gets the idea that God is the Source of his supply, and when he claims that that supply is his now, a ceaseless, tireless flow of riches becomes his here and now. Teach him his capacity to go within and weave the idea of wealth into the fabric of his mind by calling forth the spirit of opulence. You have given him wisdom. He will not want an old suit of clothes, a bowl of soup, or a dime for a cup of coffee any more. You take your bed (the truth) and walk the earth a free man when you claim what is true of God is true of you today, yesterday, and forever.

Do not see a beggar. See him as he ought to be. See him as God sees him. The disciples saw perfection, and perfection was made manifest. Do not see a cripple—see him walking and running. Let us arise to the truth of our own beingness, for becoming is really an illusion. We are perfect now. *Be ye therefore perfect (ye are perfect) even as your Father which is in Heaven is perfect.* MATT. 5:48. Let us let the scales fall from our eyes and let us claim that which was true from the foundation of the world: *Beloved, now are we the sons of God.* JOHN 3:2.

Chapter 15

(1) I am the true vine, and my Father is the husbandman. (2) Every branch in me that beareth not fruit he taketh away: and every branch that beareth fruit, he purgeth it, that it may bring forth more fruit. (3) Now ye are clean through the word which I have spoken unto you. (4) Abide in me, and I in you. As the branch cannot bear fruit of itself, except it abide in the vine; no more can ye, except ye abide in me. (5) I am the vine, ye are the branches: He that abideth in me, and I in him, the same bringeth forth much fruit: for without me ye can do nothing. (6) If a man abideth not in me, he is cast forth as a branch, and is withered; and men gather them, and cast them into the fire, and they are burned. (7) If ye abide in me, and my words abide in you, ye shall ask what ye will, and it shall be done unto you. (8) Herein is my Father glorified, that ye bear much fruit; so shall ye be my disciples. (9) As the Father hath loved me, so have I loved you: continue ye in my love. (10) If ye keep my commandments, ye shall abide in my love; even as I have kept my Father's commandments, and abide in his love.

God is the true vine, for I AM means God, and all men are rooted in God or Life. For example, every man is rooted in you, since life gives birth to all of us. The Life-Principle is One and Indivisible. It was never born and it will never die. We receive our life, our strength, and substance from God. His Life is our life; His Power is our power. It is the one Being appearing as the many. Look to the God-Presence within for your thoughts, guidance, and health. Feel and know you are rooted in the Divine from whom all blessings flow.

Branches of a tree derive their vital nourishment from a tree. If you cut the branch off, it withers and dies. It is severed from the root. The branches live as they receive sap which comes up from the vine. In the psychological sense the branches are our thoughts, desires, yearnings, and aspirations. Our ideals and desires must be rooted in consciousness; i.e., they must be sustained by the feeling of at-one-ment, or love; then they will bring forth fruit. They will become objectified as desirable conditions, events, and circumstances in our lives. If you fail to see that the solution to your problem is in your own mind, you have actually severed yourself psychologically from the Divine Center and no answer comes.

Do not wander away by becoming obsessed with forms, shapes, and the laws appertaining to matter. Learn the way of the inner man and your inner powers. You can drink of the wine of heaven by mentally claiming strength, confidence, and peace of mind. You can exchange these moods anywhere in God's universe for health, wealth, and true expression. Your faculties, talents, and desires are also branches stemming forth from the depths of yourself. Use or lose is the law of life. If we fail to use our talents for music, singing, or any other quality, these desires die within us and we become frustrated and unhappy. If you do not use your muscles, they atrophy.

Use the constructive ideas which come to you in your business, scientific, and spiritual activities. Many people working behind the bench or at the desk have wonderful ideas, plans, and dreams. These dreams and aspirations never see the light of day because they are full of fear. They look at the obstacles and delays in their mind, or sometimes they are afraid of ridicule or criticism, and their wonderful ideas which would bless the organization they are working for die within.

There are tremendous opportunities waiting for you now. Go within and draw out the precious jewels of life and with zeal and enthusiasm move forward to triumph and achievement. Stop demoting and criticizing yourself, When you do, you criticize God. Become aware of and enter into the acceptance of your good and you will expand along all lines.

Every branch that beareth fruit, he purgeth, means that every time your prayer is answered, you have gained a victory. The effects of true prayer last forever, and you are permanently cleansed of a false belief. Now you are capable of bringing forth more fruit. You can conquer through the dynamics of prayer.

Look upon prayer as a gathering together of your thoughts, attitudes, and qualities in the Presence of the King of Kings, the Lord of Lords, and singing the song of thanks and triumph. In this manner you gather yourself in the garment or mood of love which is a oneness with your desires. When your prayer is answered, you are satisfied with yourself for awhile; then another desire comes, telling you to rise higher. You meet another challenge in your mind and you have another goal to attain. You are here to go from glory to glory. The push of life is constant; there is no end to your onward march. You must experience a constant cleansing of the mind so that you may experience higher levels of awareness.

Every man who lives might be considered as a branch of the Tree of Life. I AM is the tree. All men live, move, and have their being in it. The two and one-half billion people that walk the earth are branches of God. They do not, however, bring forth fruit (harmony, peace, and joy) unless they are rooted in the Vine. The sap (inspiration, guidance, and power) is then able to come to them from God within. Without this knowledge, man accomplishes nothing. His sense of isolation, separating him from the One Power, continues. The Inner Voice is constantly urging man to go forward to do, to be, and to have. Man listens to the verdict and announcement of his senses which condemn him to the prison of fear, worry, or impotency. The outer world says, "You can't." The inner world says, "You can." Who is going to win? You determine that. If you listen to the voice of failure, it will criticize, condemn, and accuse you. You will sink into despondency and remorse.

Begin now to hear the soft tread of the unseen guest of your heart, your desire. Open your mind and heart and let in your heart's desire. Welcome it! Say, "This is from God, a message of inspiration, and new life." This is God letting you accept your good enthusiastically and lovingly. The embodiment of your inner urges will take place in response to such faith and devotion on your part.

Give up your limited concept of yourself and realize you are, by design, one with the Universal. You are rooted in the Tree of Life which grows in the midst of the garden. You are the garden of God in which you plant your seeds, such as thoughts, feelings, and

beliefs. Use the power and faculties you have. Inertia
and non-use bring stagnation, frustration, disintegra-
tion, and deterioration.

*Ye are clean through the word which I have spoken
unto you.* 15:3.

We cleanse our mind through daily meditation,
prayer, and affirming the fact that God is the Only
Presence and the Only Power. As we consciously
affirm whole-heartedly the Truths of God, these sink
down into our subliminal depths where we experience a cleansing. The Light of God, i.e., the spiritual
vibrations, destroy all the negative patterns of the
subconscious mind. The Truths of God are called the
soldiers of God which destroy thousands of negative
thought-patterns lodged in our subjective depths.

I AM is the Christmas tree with all its fruitage. The
most wonderful fruit in the world is hanging thereon
as the free gifts of God offered to all men. Man must
rise and take these gifts. Are you eating of the fruit of
the spirit?

*The fruit of the Spirit is love, joy, peace, long-
suffering, gentleness, goodness, faith, Meekness, temper-
ance: against such there is no law.* GAL. 5:22–3.

*Say ye to the righteous, that it shall be well with him:
for they shall eat the fruit of their doings. Woe unto the
wicked! it shall be ill with him: for the reward of his
hands shall be given him.* ISA. 3:10–11.

If ye abide in me, and my words abide in you, ye shall ask what ye will, and it shall be done unto you. JOHN 15:7.

These words mean that we always demonstrate whatever we have in consciousness. The way to build our desire in consciousness is to take a lively interest in it, think about it clearly, and with warm feeling. This is not excitement but a perfect confidence that what you prayed for now is. The great secret is to assume now that which you want to be. As the outside always reflects the inside, your assumption will take form and conform to the inner mold. We glorify the Father when we radiate peace, health, and happiness.

The main highlights of the rest of the chapter will now be elaborated on, omitting as much as possible the materials previously covered.

Greater love hath no man than this, that a man lay down his life for his friends. Ye are my friends, if ye do whatsoever I command you. 15:13–14.

You are commanded to let your light shine expressing health, harmony, peace, and joy. These are your greatest friends. Are you friendly and on good terms with God? Ask yourself, "What would befriend me now?" If you are sick, your greatest friend is health. Therefore you must *lay down your life for your friend.* It means you must die to the belief in sickness and disease and rise in confidence, knowledge, and trust in perfect health as the gift of God. Begin to think positively of a perfect body, building a vivid picture of yourself doing and accomplishing what you always were wont to do; then you are laying down your life for your friend. In other words, you are giving life to the idea of perfect health.

Your attention is the key to life. Give your attention to the idea of health and happiness which will pay enormous dividends. Become absorbed in the consciousness of health. You cannot afford to think of health for a few minutes; then think of discord for a few minutes; this only results in neutralization. For this reason many people do not express health and happiness. They are not one-pointed in their vision. If poverty-stricken and unable to buy the necessities of life, your friend would be the consciousness of God's abundance and wealth which would gravitate to you.

Ye have not chosen me, but I have chosen you. 15:16.

Supposing you are elected head of an organization or made the president of your club—it was your state of consciousness which determined the appointment. In other words, it is a manifestation of your inner consciousness. No experience or honor comes to you except your own mental attitude or conviction attracts it. The selection of you and the voting for you as president of your club were simply the external motions confirming and bearing witness of your exalted mood and inner belief. When you accept something as true, Infinite Intelligence acts on the minds and hearts of others causing them to aid you in the realization of your dream. The actions of others toward you bear witness to your state of consciousness. If the fruit of the tree is rotten, there is something wrong with the tree; likewise if you are experiencing lack and limitation, you must change the vine. I AM is the vine. You must go within and change your consciousness, and as your change your mental attitude and estimate of yourself, you change your experiences, conditions, and events. There is no one to change but yourself!

Whatsoever ye shall ask of the Father in my name, he may give it you. 15:16.

Whatsoever you ask means whatever you claim or believe as true will come to pass. The name means the naturalness of the state sought or the mental atmosphere of acceptance. If all we had to say was, "In the name of Jesus rise and walk," we would perform miracles. Obviously there is another meaning. *Asking in the name of Jesus* means feeling the reality of the fulfilled desire in your own consciousness. Have the consciousness of your own ability and capacity to achieve and you will not be easily thwarted from your goal.

If I had not come and spoken unto them, they had not had sin: but now they have no cloke for their sin. 15:22.

This means if you have no target to shoot at, you have no mark to miss, and you do not sin. Jesus is your Good or God in the form of your desire. Food comes to you as God when you are hungry. Water comes to you as God when you are thirsty. Likewise desires, ideas, and urges come to you from God; all you have to do is to accept them. If you have no desire to grow and demonstrate, you have nothing to shoot at. Your sin is missing your objective, the desirable state. You have no cloak for your sin because you can have no pretense, alibi, or excuse for missing the mark when you understand the law of life. The failure to realize your desire is your sin. If you are satisfied and have no desire to transcend your present concept, you remain as you are in perhaps a sick, frustrated state.

But when the Comforter is come, whom I will send unto you from the Father, even the Spirit of truth, which proceedeth from the Father, he shall testify of me. 15:26.

The positive feeling of being what you want to be is the Spirit of Truth. This is the inner testament which tells you that you are right. You are always testifying to your state of consciousness. A man who is quarrelsome by nature says, "I will move elsewhere; the people are nice there." He goes to this other place and in a short time is quarreling with everyone again.

He must get rid of the negative, mental attitude and substitute for it friendly, loving thoughts.

The Law of Life is within you, and through your thought-life you can establish contact with the inner world of the spirit and mind. Do not permit negative, defeatist thoughts to cover God's treasures within. The way of prayer is through substitution. In order for you to change, you must change ideas. You do this when you get a new perspective, a new set of spiritual values, a new spiritual standard by which you judge all thoughts, concepts, opinions, and suggestions. After reading and studying this chapter you should have a new yardstick by which to measure all thoughts and ideas which come to your mind.

Begin now to feel the Presence of God in all your transactions and in all your problems. Your new idea of life teaches you that the only way you can drive a negative thought from your mind is to supplant it with a positive, constructive thought. This is the key to health, wealth, and prosperity. The practice of these simple truths will give you faith, hope, and confidence. Go out on the limb with God—go out all the way. Have implicit trust. Have faith in God's eternal, unfailing supply of health, wealth, and all things. This faith will magnify, grow, and expand in a wonderful way. Negative states dwelt upon are also magnified and multiplied. Your state of mind is your wealth; it is the coin of the spiritual realm.

Your mood of faith and confidence in God Almighty will purchase for you anywhere, even to the ends of the earth, health, peace, joy, happiness, security, and abundance of God's riches. Having the dominant feeling of oneness with God you can buy your way any place. It opens for you all doors and wherever you go, you find yourself welcome. You find all your needs met; you paid for them with a grateful heart. Men, women, and children aid you in the journey of life because they see you coming and they say, "Behold, here comes a son of the Living God." Let us bear witness and testify that we are the sons of God. *The sons of God shouted for joy.* JOB, 38:7.

Chapter 16

(1) These things have I spoken unto you, that ye should not be offended. (2) They shall put you out of the synagogues: yea, the time cometh, that whosoever killeth you will think that he doeth God service. (3) And these things will they do unto you, because they have not known the Father, nor me. (4) But these things have I told you, that when the time shall come, ye may remember that I have told you of them. And these things I said not unto you at the beginning, because I was with you. (5) But now I go my way to him that sent me; and nine of you asketh me, Whither goes thou? (6) But because I have said these things unto you, sorrow hath filled your heart. (7) Nevertheless I tell you the truth; It is expedient for you that I go away: for if I go not away, the Comforter will not come unto you; but if I depart, I will send him unto you. (8) And when he is come, he will reprove the world of sin, and of righteousness, and of judgment: (9) Of sin, because they believe not on me; (10) Of righteousness, because I go to

*my Father, and ye see me no more; (11) Of judg-
ment, because the prince of this world is judged.
(12) I have yet many things to say unto you, but ye
cannot bear them now.*

*Whatsoever killeth you will think that he doeth
god service. 16:2.*

Many people are offended by the truth. When
you tell them that when they say, "I AM—that is
God"—they are shocked. They have God away up in
the skies, an anthropomorphic being who will judge
them on the last day. People are constantly slaying
or killing the truth of being. When you hate, resent,
quarrel, or become fearful, you are killing love, peace,
health, and happiness. You should slay ignorance, fear,
and superstition. These false concepts should die and
be slain by the sword of truth and illumined reason.
If you fear danger, failure, disease, old age, and misfortune, you are murdering—i.e., psychologically you
are separating yourself from God's Love, Light, Truth,
and Beauty. We must light the lamp in our synagogue
(our mind) and keep it burning with zeal and enthusiasm. The various religious wars down through the

centuries set forth the fact that many people thought they were doing God a favor by burning heretics and by torturing unbelievers. They were under the impression that they were actually doing God a service.

In verse seven where it says, "It is expedient for you that I go away," infers the desire must die or go away before the Comforter will come. As long as you have the desire, there is no peace. When the desire goes away or is buried as a reality in your subconscious, you are then relaxed and at peace. It is then that the Comforter comes, meaning the answered prayer which is the Peace of God. *The Comforter* is the God-Presence which is always with you. It is forever virgin, pure, unsullied. It is never tarnished or dimmed by your false beliefs and erroneous impressions. It is always waiting for you to call it. God's peace is within. God's Healing Presence is within you.

Jesus departed means that your desire disintegrates. The desire must die before you can experience it. When you have the consciousness of possession or the feeling of being what you long to be, your prayer is answered. You cannot seek what you have; you must first have it in consciousness. As long as you desire something, it means you have not accepted it in your mind as yet. When you achieve your goal through prayer, you have reproved or rejected the former limited state (sin).

Many people have a false sense of righteousness. They think by adhering to certain rules, codes, rituals, and ceremonies of a church, they are being righteous. Their judgment is also false as it is not based on laws of mind and the way of the Spirit. All prayer is an inner movement of mind and heart. If you want health, feed the mind with premises which are true. Take your attention away from the condition you do not want and place it upon health and harmony. Have a perfect picture of health; fill in the picture with confidence and faith in the Healing Presence. Instruct your mind with all the reasons why you can have health. As you continue to do this regularly, you will succeed in impressing your consciousness with the deep conviction of health. This is true righteousness or right use of the laws of mind and not the righteousness of the Scribes and Pharisees who believe God is punishing them or disease is sent to make them suffer.

Your judgement is true because it is based on spiritual standards and the will of God which must be something beyond your wildest dreams. You can rise above the fear of anything now. Perhaps you are worried about a loved one or a sick friend. You can change your mind; then the condition is changed. You now have fear at your mercy. Your mind is saturated with confidence; you continue in this mental state, and your faith grows in strength until finally your mind unites with its good. You have now pronounced judgment on the prince of this world as mentioned in verse eleven. *The prince of this world* refers to race belief, negative suggestions, plus the avalanche of sights and sounds which come to us from the outside world. The judgment you come to about the prince of the world is a complete mental rejection of all negative thoughts which are only shadows of the mind. When your mind is consciously controlled, directed, and disciplined to perceive only the good, you have pronounced judgment on the false beliefs and fears of the mind; you have executed or killed the false concepts and rendered a verdict in favor of your good. (This was the way Quimby prayed for people.)

In verse twelve you have a profound mystical statement of truth. You can only hear what you are ready to receive. The average five-sense-man taking the Bible literally is not always ready or equal to grasping the psychological or inner meaning of life. The mind of man must be open, receptive, ready, and eager to hear and know. You cannot teach a ten year old boy all about chemistry in one lesson. It takes years of preparation, study, and research. The usual procedure is to absorb this inner teaching of the Bible by degrees. The teacher of the laws of mind realizes that the student is not ready to receive many things which he wishes to impart to him. Some of the race beliefs and the literal understanding of the Bible are so imbedded in our minds that our attitude often implies, "It is too good to be true," because the inner, concealed, esoteric meaning of the Bible contradicts almost everything the average man has ever heard.

The following verses which we will explain represent the meat or essence of the rest of chapter sixteen.

Howbeit when he, the Spirit of truth, is come, he will guide you into all truth: for he shall not speak of himself; but whatsoever he shall hear, that shall he speak: and he will shew you things to come. 16:13.

The Spirit of truth is intuition and inspiration which well up within us. Infinite Intelligence responds to the demand made upon Itself. It is both the question and the answer. If you become still and think of God and His Wisdom, your mind moves from worry and fear to a deep, quiet subconscious faith. The Inner Light is beginning to shine on you now. Listen for the voice of God, the divine ideas will well up when the surface mind is calm. The answer may come as a flash of illumination, as the Still Small Voice, or a silent inner knowing.

A woman when she is in travail hath sorrow, because her hour is come: but as soon as she is delivered of the child, she remembereth no more the anguish, for joy that a man is born into the world. 16:21.

Haven't you noticed that when you pray, sometimes conditions seem to get worse. The house topples down around us, so to speak. It is like sweeping a house, you create a lot of dust. You are suffering or undergoing travail for the joy that is set before you. This is a sure sign that the law is working and that you are giving birth to your child (ideal, desire, plan). Prayer changes the subconscious mind, and you must remember the derelicts of fear, confusion, and error fight to retain their stronghold on your deeper mind. You create a little turmoil in dislodging them. Before something is born, something is destroyed. Many people, though they are about ninety per cent through the tunnel, often turn back; if they had persisted a few more days, they would have seen the light of the new day. Ofttimes prayer is like going through a tunnel, we find it is pitch black. If we continue on, we will come out the other end.

In prayer we get rid of a lot of dirty linen in the subconscious mind. The process seems to be creating a lot of chaos. The woman (subconscious) seems to be in travail. As soon as she is delivered of child (as soon as our prayer is objectified), she remembers not the anguish. All is forgotten in the joy of the answered prayer. This is the meaning of the phrase in verse twenty-two, *And your joy no man taketh from you.*

Hitherto have ye asked nothing in my name: ask, and ye shall receive, that your joy may be full. 16:24.

Many seem to think that if they ask in the name of Jesus Christ that their prayer will be answered. You are Jesus Christ or the spiritual man in action when you know that you cannot experience anything but that which you have accepted in your mind or consciousness. You are Jesus Christ when your conscious and subconscious mind agree on the reality of your wish or prayer. When there is no further argument, and you have reached an agreement, you are Jesus Christ in action—Jesus representing your illumined reason, and Christ the Power of the subjective self.

Know ye not your own selves, how that Jesus Christ is in you, except ye be reprobates? II Cor. 13:5.

Your idea and feeling must agree or your mind must blend with your heart; then you are in agreement, and your prayer will be answered. The name of anything means the nature, character, properties, or attributes of a thing. If I call you by name, you respond. If I call in faith, good responds.

I told a young lady recently who wanted to be a teacher of the laws of mind to assume the role of a teacher in her consciousness. In her imagination she began to teach and dramatize the truth to a large body of students. She felt the thrill of all this until it became a part of her. She studied, attended classes, took courses for a practitioner in some of the schools, also studied for the ministerial course. She told me all her teachers said to her that she had transcended them. All the attributes and qualities necessary to become an outstanding teacher were resurrected within her. This is asking in the name or nature of the desire by appropriating the idea, and feasting upon it, so that it became a part of her, as food becomes a part of our natural body.

In the world ye shall have tribulation: but be ye of good cheer; I have overcome the world. 16:33.

Our mind is a receptive medium for all the propaganda, opinions, and erroneous impressions coming from the world outside. There are good and bad impressions. Except, however, man's mind is deliberately and wisely trained to sift the chaff from the wheat, the bad and erroneous impressions take root and cause trouble, such as sickness, confusion, fear, and limitation of all kinds. The world believes in good and evil, sickness and lack. If we remain in these worldly beliefs and neglect scientific prayer, we shall have tribulations, trials, and difficulties.

Be of good cheer; let your knowledge of the Infinite One overcome all your problems. Begin now to fill your mind with the Eternal Verities. Become aware of your inherent, God-given powers which enable you to give attention, devotion, and love to ideas which heal, bless, inspire, elevate, dignify, and fill your soul with joy. You move in the direction of your dominant state of consciousness. Your awareness of God's Powers and His Presence filling your soul enables you to soar aloft over all obstacles to the haven of the spiritual realm where you rest in the conviction that with God all things are possible. Maintaining this attitude of mind in the presence of difficulties will enable you to overcome the world (objective conditions and worldly fears). You shall be like the one spoken of by the prophet: *And he shall be like a tree planted by the rivers of water, that bringeth forth his fruit in his season; his leaf also shall not wither; and whatsoever he doeth shall prosper.* Ps. 1:3.

Chapter 17

(1) These words spake Jesus, and lifted up his eyes to heaven, and said, Father, the hour is come, glorify thy Son, that thy Son also may glorify thee: (2) As thou hast given him power over all flesh, that he should give eternal life to as many as thou hast given him. (3) And this is life eternal, that they might know thee the only true God, and Jesus Christ, whom thou hast sent. (4) I have glorified thee on the earth: I have finished the work which thou gavest me to do. (5) And now, O Father, glorify thou me with thine own self with the glory which I had with thee before the world was. (6) I have manifested thy name unto the men which thou gavest me out of the world: thine they were, and thou gavest them me; and they have kept thy word. (7) Now they have known that all things whatsoever thou hast given me are of thee. (8) For I have given unto them the words which thou gavest me; and they have received them, and have known surely that I came out from thee, and they have believed that thou didst send me. (9) I pray for them: I pray

not for the world, but for them which thou hast given me; for they are thine. (10) And all mine are thine, and thine are mine; and I am glorified in them. (11) And now I am no more in the world, but these are in the world, and I come to thee. Holy Father, keep through thine own name those whom thou hast given me, that they may be one, as we are. (12) While I was with them in the world, I kept them in thy name: those that thou gavest me I have kept, and none of them is lost, but the son of perdition; that the scripture might be fulfilled.

This prayer is known as the great awakening—man awakening to his splendor and glory as a son of God. Herein is portrayed the union of man with God, or the perfect blending of the intellect with the Wisdom of God. *The hour is come* means the death of all limitation and an awakening to your oneness in God and all things good. When man has completely purified his subconscious mind and when his conscious mind is free from all fear and sense of limitation, the two become one. The hour comes when you enter the state of consciousness revealing your unity

with the whole. Through a sort of Interior awareness, man perceives instantaneously the great Truths
of God. He then desires to glorify, make magnificent, each mental conception he conceives. His son
(or conception) must reflect this glorification back to
his Father-Creator. The *son* is every man; you really
glorify the Father when you manifest health, peace,
harmony, understanding, and good will. When your
intellect is illumined by the Wisdom of God, you are
also glorifying your Father. *To glorify* means to exalt,
magnify, praise, and to enhance spiritually. *You have
power over all flesh* means you have dominion over
your world.

The word *flesh* infers your body, environment,
five-sense-evidence, race belief, and world-thought.
You must realize that the Spiritual Power within you
is your Lord, It is your master and responds to your
thought. You don't make an effect a cause. You are cog-
nizant of your spiritual dominion and your authority
over your body and environment. Your body is completely subject to your command. It has no volition or
initiative of itself; it is governed by inertia. The Self-
Mover is within you. Your body moves as it is moved
upon. It acts as it is acted upon. You have power over
all flesh or man-made opinions. You can keep alive
wrong, negative images, or turn your attention to the
more harmonious mental concepts, and by power of

the mind keep them alive. True glorification is Cosmic Consciousness and expansion into the Divine.

In verse four *I have finished* the work means that I now reclaim all the former power and glory as the son of God. When you pray, you finish the work by going within and visioning yourself as possessing what you long to possess or expressing what you long to express.

I told an alcoholic a few weeks ago to imagine his wife congratulating him and to keep on believing that picture in his mind. I explained to him that he would draw power from the subconscious mind which would take away all craving and compel him to express his freedom from the habit. This mental picture was objectified in his experience, and a new habit-pattern had been established. He had finished his work; i.e., he gradually built up his consciousness through thinking and feeling of his freedom until finally his consciousness became full, the quality of his moods, and what he declared and felt inside became a function and a real experience.

You finish your work when you go within and subjectify your prayer through your confidence in the Powers of the Law. God willed the world to man, but man is asleep to his Inner Powers. Man is heir to all that is. *I am the light of the world.* JOHN 9:15.

Some men are conscious of being one hundred watt, others two hundred, five hundred, etc., but when man awakens to the fact that he is one with Limitless Light, he is no longer limited. Electricity is not conscious of being light—it is. We come here to remember, and when we fully remember who we are and from whence we came, the works are really finished. Troward says, "All things are made by the self-contemplation of spirit." God contemplated Himself as man, so He became man.

In verse seven where it says, "All things whatsoever thou hast given me are of thee," means that all things man ever experienced came to him through his own consciousness. The instant man believes his prayer is answered, he must see it appear in the world of form. We are here on a voyage of self discovery. We are here to discover who we are. "Pilgrim, pilgrimage, and road was but a journey from myself to myself." The seeming many merely tell me who I am.

Verse ten, *All mine are thine, and thine are mine; and I am glorified in them*, means that God is all there is, and what is true of God is true of man because man is God made manifest. All of God's Wisdom, Intelligence, and Power is within each man awaiting his discovery and use. Our consciousness is one and indestructible; all things and experiences come from consciousness, and all things return to consciousness. You become glorified when you really become a channel through which God's Light and Love flow freely. This Vast Motionless Being which men call God is limited by belief in being someone. Every child born is the Universal Life appearing as that child. It is God being born, and every child is born in the race belief and to all that his environment represents.

While I was with them in the world, I kept them in thy name: those that thou gavest me I have kept, and none of them is lost, but the son of perdition; that the scripture might be fulfilled. 17:12.

Verse twelve means that I keep all things in thy name by claiming, "I am that thing." You keep all your mental images *fixed in thy name*, meaning that you feel the naturalness and reality of what you pray for. The word *name* means the nature or naturalness of the thing prayed for. *The son of perdition* means the belief in loss, the sense of limitation. The only loss is belief in loss, and once this belief in loss dies, there is no loss. The son of perdition also means the belief in loss of the soul. No man or thing can be lost. We see in this verse that the belief in loss must go so that the scripture might be fulfilled with the knowledge that man's consciousness is God and that his own consciousness is his savior. There is no lost soul for the simple reason God can't lose Himself.

We will now dwell on the high lights of the remaining verses in this chapter.

I have given them thy word; and the world hath hated them, because they are not of the world, even as I am not of the world. 17:14.

The world for centuries with its belief in its material gods has discredited the idea that man's consciousness first creates all things mentally; then he sees them materialize. *I am not of the world,* means I AM is man's indwelling consciousness, and it has the complete Power to make its own creation without the help of any man. This basic principle will be the foundation of the new mental world which is about to blossom forth.

I pray not that thou shouldest take them out of the world, but that thou shouldest keep them from evil. 17:15.

We do not have to retire into a monastery or isolate ourselves from people in order to live spiritually. To run away is escapism. We do not run away from life, but we stand our ground, and say, "Fear not, I have overcome the world." We can prove our divinity on Times Square or Hollywood Boulevard. We can grow spiritually in a large city just as well as in a mountain retreat.

And for their sake I sanctify myself, that they also might be sanctified through truth.

We must realize that there is no one to change but ourselves. As man changes his estimate or concept of himself, he changes his relationship to the world. We must sanctify ourselves—that is, we make ourselves whole and pure. If I first sanctify myself, I see only the pure, only the good in my mind.

For example, suppose I want peace in the world, I must start with myself. As I establish peace in my own mind, I will contribute to the peace of the whole world. If I am friendly with the God-Self within, I will be friendly with all men who walk the earth. "As within, so without." When I look through the eyes of love, I cannot hate the meanest man in the world. I cannot see other than the contents of my consciousness. If I am identified with the lovely and the good, I cannot see the unlovely. To the pure all things are pure. I cannot experience harmony in the external plane, until I first have established a harmonious, mental atmosphere within myself. The judgment or conviction of others is to oneself. Whatever you are thinking about the other, you are thinking about yourself. Cease trying to change the world; change yourself. The world is ourselves in aggregation. The dictators, despots, and tyrants of the world are extensions in space of the dictator-complexes in the minds and hearts of all of us.

That they all may be one; as thou, Father, art in me, and I in thee, that they also may be one in us: that the world may believe that thou hast sent me. And the glory which thou gavest me I have given them; that they may be one, even as we are one. 17:21-2.

These verses set forth the great truth that there is only one thing to worship, one thing to seek, and that is the consciousness of God's Presence. All things are made inside and out of this Power and Presence. It is One and Indivisible. In reality we are one.

By illustration, if we look at the continents, they seem to be divided; yet underneath the ocean is one uniting all of them. We see projections of dry land on top of the one ocean. Objectively we seem to be different and separate individuals; however Mind and Life is One and Indivisible. Subjectively we are all one. Everything you look at is the One Being appearing as rock, sand, sun, moon, trees, animals, etc. All men are extensions of yourself.

Consider all the hairs of your head and all the cells of your body; millions of cells seem to make your body; likewise the two and a half billion people in the world are like the cells of your body; they are extension of yourself. If I hurt another, I hurt myself. If I help another, I am helping myself. We are all one. This is why we say, "Our Father," proving we are all brothers and sisters. It is One Being dramatizing Himself as the many. Claim the highest and greatest concept of self.

I in them, and thou in me, but that they may be made perfect in one. 17:23.

This verse reminds us of a great truth pointing out that no matter what the eyes tell us conditions may be, we must be blind to all except the perfect state we want to see. We must ask in the consciousness that no matter what we pray for, it is so.

And I have declared unto them thy name, and will declare it: that the love wherewith thou hast loved me may be in them, and I in them. 17:26.

This means that all through the ages teachers have declared the Truth: I AM the Lord, I AM the door, and I AM is the only law of consciousness. Millions of years from now this Truth will still be declared, until mankind becomes aware of the being he really is. As this love of Truth is made known to the individual, he loves this Eternal Principle and enjoys sharing this Divine secret with his brother man. Sooner than we think will the Fatherhood of God and the brotherhood of man be made manifest in this entire earth-conscious planet.

Chapter 18

(1) When Jesus had spoken these words, he went forth with his disciples over the brook Cedron, where was a garden, into the which he entered, and his disciples. (2) And Judas also, which betrayed him, knew the place: for Jesus ofttimes resorted thither with his disciples. (3) Judas then, having received a band of men and officers from the chief priests and Pharisees, cometh thither with lanterns and torches and weapons. (4) Jesus therefore, knowing all things that should come upon him, went forth, and said unto them, Whom seek ye? (5) They answered him, Jesus of Nazareth. Jesus saith unto them, I am he. And Judas also, which betrayed him, stood with them. (6) As soon then as he had said unto them, I am he, they went backward, and fell to the ground. (7) Then asked he them again, Whom seek ye? And they said, Jesus of Nazareth. (8) Jesus answered, I have told you that I am he: if therefore ye seek me, let these go their way: (9) That the saying might be fulfilled, which he spake, Of them which

*thou gavest me have I lost none. (10) Then Simon
Peter having a sword drew it, and smote the high
priest's servant, and cut off his right ear. The servant's name was Malchus.*

You are in the garden of your mind when you
meditate on *Whatsoever things are true, whatsoever
things are honest, whatsoever things are lovely, whatsoever things are of good report; if there be any virtue,
and if there be any praise, think of these things.* PHIL.
4:8: When you are dwelling and concentrating on the
above mentioned great truths, you are in the garden of
Gethsemane where you are truly pressing out the oil
of gladness and joy.

In verse four and five the question, *Whom seek ye?*
means that we are always seeking Jesus, or the thing
that would save us. The only way we can receive our
good is on the basis of our understanding of the laws
of mind and our consciousness of complete acceptance. The voice answered, "I am he."

In verse six it says, *As soon then as he had said
unto them, I am he, they went backward, and fell to the
ground.* We do not, of course, take this literally. From
a literal standpoint it makes little or no sense. It is not

referring to a group of men with torches and weapons falling on the ground at the sight of a gentle man in prayer. We must not get lost in the peculiarities and idiosyncrasies of literalisms. The only way these stories of the Bible will help you is by seeing the real spiritual values behind the words; then all your erroneous concepts, false theories, negative and fearful thoughts fall to the ground; i.e., they are cast out of your mind and lose all their power.

They went backward, means you have forsaken the false concepts and you have enthroned the recognition and allegiance to the One Supreme, Spiritual Presence called I AM in the Bible. The word he (I am he) is a later interpolation. You can enter into the garden of Gethsemane as you read these pages. Quiet your mind, sit still, focus all your attention on your desire or goal, and be faithful to your objective. If you find your attention wandering, bring it back to the contemplation of your ideal and its reality.

If therefore ye seek me, let these go their way. 18:8. When seeking a solution to your problem you acknowledge no other Power than God and you disavow and reject all beliefs in other powers. Your mind is disciplined and you are completely absorbed in the contemplation of the reality of your desire.

In verse ten the *cutting off of the right ear* symbolizes that we refuse to listen to objective evidences, outward appearances, or to outer descriptions and viewpoints of other people.

Then said Jesus unto Peter, Put up thy sword into the sheath: the cup which my Father hath given me, shall I not drink it? 18:11.

The cup is your mind which is receptive to the idea. You pour coffee into a cup; similarly pour life, love, feeling, and enthusiasm into your idea. Every seed is a promise of fruit or food depending on its nature. Your desire is a prophecy of its own fulfillment. All that is necessary is mental receptivity.

Then the band and the captain and officers of the Jews took Jesus, and bound him, And led him away to Annas first; for he was father in law to Caiaphas, which was the high priest that same year. 18:12–13.

Annas (intellect, conscious mind) is father-in-law to *Caiaphas* (which means father in the law). The law is: *I am that which I feel myself to be. Caiaphas* means pit, a hollowed out part, or the subconscious mind. The conscious mind is father to the subconscious because it controls the subconscious and impregnates it with all kinds of impressions.

It was expedient that one man should die for the people . . . (18:14) means that Jesus or our desire must die first before it can be resurrected.

Except a corn of wheat fall into the ground and die, it abideth alone: but if it die, it bringeth forth much fruit.

12:24. Troward says the seed (your desire) has its own mathematics and mechanics with it, i.e., the desire you have contains within itself its own manner of realization and fulfillment. When you feel and believe you are now what you long to be, you have died to your former concept or estimate of yourself and you have resurrected the new concept.

In the prayer-process you detach your consciousness from the problem or difficulty and you vividly dwell on the reality of your desire knowing that it will reproduce itself in your world. You mentally let go of all the things which held you in bondage and you begin to live mentally with that which you wish to embody in your world. Whatever you are aware of now represents your faith. You are aware of the reality of what you are praying for as you read this chapter and you positively, definitely, incisively, and decisively no longer give power to externals; neither do you postulate other powers, barriers, and opposition to your ideals.

I had the interesting experience with a man suffering from functional paralysis. I told him to make a vivid picture of himself walking around his office, touching the desk, answering the telephone, and doing all the things he ordinarily would do if he were healed. He lived the role and actually felt himself back in his office. One day, after several weeks of prayer along the above lines, the telephone rang and kept ringing (it was all arranged by the writer); his wife and nurse were out. The telephone was about twelve feet away, and he answered the telephone. His wife knew he was healed at that hour. The Almighty Power flowed to the focal point of his attention, and a healing followed. Psychologically speaking, the mental picture was developed in the dark house of his mind and a complete healing followed. This man had a mental block which prevented impulses from the brain reaching his legs; therefore he said he could not walk.

When man shifts his attention to the Healing Power of the Omnipotent One, the Power flows and dissolves everything unlike Itself. He completely died to his former belief of a crippled state and began to live to that which he claimed as true. In Biblical language he, like Judas (problem, sickness, lack) committed suicide or died to the old state, and the Jesus, or saving state of consciousness, was resurrected. He took life from the old state by refocusing his attention on the new state and living in the mental atmosphere as though it was true; this state of consciousness finally jelled within him. You could say in the language of the Bible that he went out and committed suicide (death of old state).

No man taketh it (my life) *from me . . . I have power to lay it down, and I have power to take it again.* 10:18.

In the same manner you must die to what you are before you can live to what you wish to be.

We are taking highlights of the balance of this chapter which represents the essence of it. We are told in verse twenty-seven that Peter denied Jesus. A similar story appears in Matthew 26:34. *Before the cock crow, thou shalt deny me thrice.* This means that every man should deny having any master other than God or the Spiritual Power within. The numeral three represents a deep, abiding, faith or conviction. As long as we have masters, other powers, or beliefs which dominate or control us, we are slaves. Many are slaves to the weather and the unseen virus, blaming the latter for their influenza or grippe.

Peter denies three times means that state of consciousness in you, or the disciplined attitude, which will permit only faith in the One Power and the One Presence and is not subject to any other powers. *To deny three times* is a subjective state of belief which does not allow any argument. After the creative act and always at dawn the cock crows heralding the birth of the sun (the illumined conscious mind). The dawn appears and the shadows of fear and doubt flee away. Peter denied Jesus (after the flesh) three times, symbolizes the song of triumph, whereby man gives supreme attention to the Lord and Master within—his own I AM-NESS as Creator and Deliverer from all problems.

(31) *Then said Pilate unto them, Take ye him, and judge him according to your law. The Jews therefore said unto him, It is not lawful for us to put any man to death:* (32) *That the saying of Jesus might be fulfilled, which he spake, signifying what death he should die.* (33) *Then Pilate entered into the judgment hall again, and called Jesus, and said unto him, Art thou the King of the Jews?* (34) *Jesus answered him, Sayest thou this thing of thyself, or did others tell it thee of me?* (35) *Pilate answered, Am I a Jew? Thine own nation and the chief priests have delivered thee unto me: what has thou done?* (36) *Jesus answered, My kingdom is not of this world: if my kingdom were of this world, then would my servants fight, that I should not be delivered to the Jews: but now is my kingdom not from hence.* (37) *Pilate therefore said unto him, Art thou a king then? Jesus answered, Thou sayest I am a king. To this end I was born, and for this cause came I into the world, that I should bear witness unto the truth. Every one that is of the truth heareth my voice.* (38) *Pilate saith unto him, What is truth? And when he had said this, he went out again unto the Jews, and saith unto them, I find in him no fault at all.* (39) *But ye have a custom, that I should release unto you one at the passover: will ye therefore that I release unto you the King of the Jews?* (40) *Then cried they all again, saying, Not this man, but Barabbas. Now Barabbas was a robber.*

Pilate is the conscious mind which is always passing judgment. You are passing judgment all day long based upon the thoughts you think, the decision, or conclusion arrived at in your mind. *The judgment hall* spoken of is the realm of mind which is often vague and confused.

In verse thirty-three the conscious mind does not know what salvation is because only feeling can know that. *Our servants* in verse thirty-six are our thoughts, ideas, feelings, and understanding of mental and spiritual laws. Possessing confidence and faith in the higher workings of the mind, the result is inevitable; all obstacles will dissolve and vanish away. We do not strive externally to reach a peace which comes from within. That which we get by force we have to maintain by force. Love frees; it forever gives of Itself; it is Universal; it is the Spirit of God.

In verse thirty-seven every man is a king, for the simple reason he is absolute monarch over his thoughts, emotions, and reactions to life. He can order his thoughts around. He can refuse a passport to all negative concepts and false ideas. He is king of his own conceptive realm. *Your kingdom* is your consciousness. Your edict (belief) will always be obeyed, and there is none to question it, since you have dominion over your thoughts and feelings. This verse tells us that we are here to dramatize; bear witness to God's presence, and prove we have dominion.

I told a man in our special Bible class on this Gospel he was king over alcohol and that he was master. He started imagining himself back at his desk. He kept up the constant visioning of himself as free, happy, and successfully accomplishing his former work. He knew that this constant visioning of mental pictures in his mind would draw power from his unconscious depths and compel him to be free from the habit. He fulfilled his vision by adhering to this simple truth. His vision became a concrete reality in his experience. His mental picture was transmuted into peace of mind and perfect sobriety. *In my flesh shall I see God.*

Verse thirty-eight means that the conscious, worldly-minded individual is always asking, "What is Truth?" *Truth* is always silent. It is beyond argument, dialectics, theories, dogmas, and creeds. *Truth* is an inner experiences, an inner awareness, or feeling whereby you taste and touch reality for yourself. Your consciousness determines all your experiences and your relationship with the external world and all people. The Bible says, "I am the Truth."

The Presence of God in you is the real Truth, the Changeless Reality within all of us. Truth is the subjective factor which is the real cause of all our experiences. It is no use to argue that two and two are not four. Truth permits no argument. Truth is.

I talked to a brother and sister recently. The sister broke out in a rash when she ate strawberries; however the brother liked strawberries very much and had no ill effects. The truth about the matter was, of course, a subjective fear on the part of the girl. When she ate strawberries rejoicing and affirming, "This is spiritual substance and is transmuted into beauty by my digestive system," she had no more trouble.

Every truth in this relative world is called a half-truth because it is done unto us as we believe. If you believe poison ivy will give you a severe rash, the experience becomes real to you. I have seen soldiers sleep on poison ivy without any bad reactions. What is *Truth?* It is a subjective belief. You will find confusion, argument, discord, and strife in this relative world, but deep within you the Infinite lies stretched in smiling repose. In the Absolute all is Bliss, Peace, Harmony, and Perfection. This is the Wise Silence of Emerson. God abides in the silence; Truth is lived in silence; Truth is heard in the silence; Truth is felt in the silence; Truth is transmitted in the silence, for God abides in the silence. It is wonderful!

You can enter this Secret Place of the Most High where, fashioning your own wish as already fulfilled, it is done unto you as you believe. Inspiration, guidance, and illumination come to man in the silence when he is still and alone with God. All the characters of the Bible are within yourself and should not be looked upon as historical events of two thousand years ago.

The custom of releasing one at the passover as mentioned in verse thirty-nine is the art and process of prayer. The *passover* represents the change of consciousness as you pass over from the old to the new state of awareness, in the same way as the alcoholic mentioned previously in this chapter passed from the vision of his health and happiness to the actual, concrete experience in his mind and body, whereby he expressed sobriety and peace of mind as a living fact.

The multitude (your thoughts and desires) cry, "Not this man, but Barabbas. Now Barabbas was a robber." All of us want to get rid of *Barabbas* or the state of consciousness that robs us of peace, harmony, and prosperity. If we are sick, we cry for health (Jesus—that which saves); we want to release Barabbas (sickness).

A man with colitis for one year hesitated to give up his resentment to a partner. I told him he would have a healing if he would let go the resentment (Barabbas) and fill his heart with love and good will (Jesus). His resentment was the anchor which bound him to the wheel of pain. He began to wish for his associate all of God's riches, such as peace, health, joy, life, liberty, and all good things. He had a healing. The crowd of thoughts in his mind were shouting for the release of Barabbas so that he could experience normal functioning of his organism.

If you have an unfulfilled desire, dream, or goal, you must be harboring in your mind some thoughts of fear or worry, or you are seeing barriers to its fulfillment. Identify yourself now with your goal by mentally and emotionally uniting with it. Build it up in your mind by frequently visioning its fulfillment. As you add one brick to another in the building of your house, your sustained mood or feeling will gradually grow and magnify until your consciousness is full of the quality of your thought and feeling. Having persevered and having remained faithful to your vision, you will crucify or cause your ideal to cross over from the conscious sphere of life to the subjective state of inner awareness or subconscious embodiment.

You are Pilate, Jesus, Barabbas, and the multitude, and when you have a problem, you must mentally release Barabbas and be sure to crucify your Jesus (desire). In order to realize your desire, it must be crucified; i.e., it must be fixed in consciousness. Your desire must die or be felt as true, otherwise you will continue desiring it.

Prayer is a death and birth process as we are always dying to the old and living to the new. The drama of the crucifixion is a mystical one. It is not a story of a group of people called Jews sentencing a man to death. No one can kill your savior. You are your own savior. Your faith in God is your personal savior. We have distorted and twisted this story of prayer and made of it a sadistic and blood-curdling drama. We must cease stigmatizing a race of people called Jews, and realize the whole story is a beautiful drama of man's awakening to his Godhood.

Chapter 19

(1) Then Pilate therefore took Jesus, and scourged him. (2) And the soldiers platted a crown of thorns, and put it on his head, and they put on him a purple robe. (3) And said, Hail, King of the Jews! and they smote him with their hands. (4) Pilate therefore went forth again, and saith unto them, Behold, I bring forth to you, that ye may know that I find no fault with him. (5) Then came Jesus forth, wearing the crown of thorns, and the purple robe. And Pilate saith unto them, Behold the man! (6) When the chief priests therefore and officers saw him, they cried out, saying, Crucify him, crucify him. Pilate saith unto them, Take ye him, and crucify him: for I find no fault in him. (7) The Jews answered him, We have a law, and by our law he ought to die, because he made himself the Son of God. (8) When Pilate therefore heard that saying, he was the more afraid; (9) And went forth again into the judgment hall, and saith unto Jesus, Whence art thou? But Jesus gave him no answer.

(10) Then saith Pilate unto him, Speakest thou not unto me? knowest thou not that I have power to crucify thee, and have power to release thee? (11) Jesus answered, Thou couldest have no power at all against me, except it were given thee from above; therefore he that delivered me unto thee hath the greater sin. (12) And from thenceforth Pilate sought to release him: but the Jews cried out, saying, If thou let this man go, thou art not Caesar's friend: whosoever maketh himself a king speaketh against Caesar.

The *crown of thorns* symbolizes the crown of victory or triumph which comes to all men as they move from darkness to light, from pain to peace, a sovereignty as you overcome the trials and tribulations of life. It is the victory of the spiritual man, a power molded in gentleness, love, and spiritual awareness. As you wear the garment of confidence—the Power of God over all things in your life—your perception and understanding will grow. The man of faith is always full of power. This is the ruling authority in your mind based on an abiding faith in the One Spiritual Power. Trusting and believing in One Power, you wear the diadem of the universe (the crown of thorns). Lift up your cross (your ideal or concept of God), and you will become a ruler and commander of the peoples of your mind. You are now ready to wear the purple robe, the garment of royalty or your kingship.

In verse seven the *Jews* symbolize the average man governed by old beliefs, or one who believes that because a man says he is a son of God he is a blasphemer and should be punished.

In verse ten the conscious mind has the power to crucify or impress the subconscious mind with any idea or belief through feeling. It also has the power to release or cleanse the subconscious of all negative states through prayer, meditation, and positive affirmations of God's Eternal Verities.

Verse eleven means that the conscious mind has no real power as the subjective alone is creative. All power is in the subjective mind. The conscious mind simply chooses the concept which through subjective feeling is entombed in the subjective mind, and is then given back to the conscious mind. The subjective mind will accept your convictions, beliefs, and feeling whether exalted or ignoble.

In verse twelve Caesar's power (conscious mind or worldly beliefs) is conditioned upon the feeling of the subjective. When we raise our ideal to the point of kingship, we speak against Caesar—the world. When new perceptions of truth and illumination light up our mind, we deny or reject all the false beliefs of the world thereby speaking or rejecting Caesar (world or race belief).

The world, meaning the average man's mind full of false information, viewpoints, and opinions, always challenges the real truth of things. When a man awakens to the fact that his own mind is causative and actually enters into all experiences in which he believes, that man knows the inner principle of causation; he is full of light or new understanding, and wins over the world-beliefs. He becomes the conqueror and goes forth conquering and to conquer.

The chief priests answered, We have no king but Caesar. 19:15.

The chief priests are our dominant beliefs or ideas looking to external powers, believing in ritual, form, and ceremonies, governed by the world, conscious of outward rank, and wedded to tradition. Such men are usually unwilling to listen to the Truths of God and Life because it means an abandonment of their power and loss of their hold over the people. *The chief priests* also refer to states of consciousness within ourselves, such as pride, arrogance, self-conceit, and old theological concepts of God which we are unwilling to give up.

(17) *And he bearing his cross went forth into a place which is called the place of a skull, which is called in the Hebrew Golgotha: (18) Where they crucified him, and two others with him, on either side one, and Jesus in the midst.*

Golgotha means skull, or our own consciousness which is always the place of crucifixion. You die in Golgotha when you now vividly imagine and feel that you are what you want to be. As you continue to charge your mental imagery with interest and enthusiasm, you will succeed in etching your picture on the deeper mind, because the law is what you impress, you express; you have now died in Golgotha. You have died to the old man, and the new picture or estimate of yourself is resurrected.

The crown we bear is our ideal or new concept of ourselves. We must, of course, wear it mentally to the point of death, or subjective embodiment, or complete appropriation of the idea. You are carrying your cross for the joy that is set before you. Continue to hear the glad tidings; persevere in hearing only what you want to hear. When you rise in consciousness to the point of acceptance, the old idea dies and the new comes forth, causing a change which is referred to as the passover; this is also crucifixion.

In verse eighteen each person is represented by Jesus or your own consciousness which is always between two thieves. As you read this chapter, you are saying to yourself, "This makes sense because it is true of myself." The *two thieves* are that which you now are and that which you want or fondly desire to be; in other words, you and your desire.

If you have arthritis, for example, the pain and inflammation is one thief, and your desire for health which you have had for a long time is also a thief; for my desire, when realized, would prove to be my savior; as I continue desiring it, I am robbing myself of the joy of perfect health. *The two thieves* are with all of us, the "I am not" state and the "that which I wish to be" state. Our own consciousness (Jesus) is between these two states. One thief says, "Lord, remember me when thou comest into thy kingdom?" Luke 23:42. And the answer is, "Today shalt thou be with me in paradise." Luke 23:43. These two verses set forth the true method of prayer.

The Lord is your spiritual awareness. *To remember* is to gather yourself together mentally and turn to the One Power recognizing it as your Lord, Master, and the Supreme Creative Power. You become enthusiastic about your desire and you begin to woo it in consciousness in the same manner that an engaged couple are eager to be married. As you turn in confidence to the God-Presence, It turns to you and responds in the nature of your request; then the old pattern dies and the new is born; this is paradise or peace, a oneness with your ideal.

In verse nineteen and twenty of this chapter it says, *And Pilate wrote a title, and put it on the cross. And the writing was JESUS OF NAZARETH THE KING OF THE JEWS. And it was written in Hebrew, and Greek, and Latin.* This means the three steps in prayer. *Hebrew* means your Spiritual Power or God; *Greek* means the divine idea or desire; and *Latin* means the feeling of being what you long to be, resulting in manifestation. Hebrew represents the language of God, Greek the language of the intellect, and Latin the language of commerce. Another way of stating it is this: Hebrew means recognition of God or your consciousness as the creative power; Greek means the desire or idea in your conscious, reasoning mind; Latin means the movement or corresponding emotion generated as you meditate on the idea. This is the creative process in all answered prayers. You must give your ideas wings, animating them; thereby making them alive within you.

(23) *Then the soldiers, when they had crucified Jesus, took his garments, and made four parts, to every soldier a part; and also his coat: now the coat was without seam, woven from the top throughout. (4) They said therefore among themselves, Let us not rend it, but cast lots for it, whose it shall be: that the scripture might be*

fulfilled, which saith, They parted my raiment among them, and for my vesture they did cast lots. These things therefore the soldiers did.

These verses indicate the confused, contentious mind of the worldly, five-sense man who divides the truth into many parts; yet all the time he does not know that there can be but one truth, for there is only one God. In order for man to transform himself, he must positively discard old patterns of thinking and feeling; this is painful to him. He wants to hold on to the old. He is just as willing to die for his superstitions as he is for the truth. Man has divided the seamless robe (the one God, the one Truth) and created countless false gods. He has even polluted the atmosphere with his strange notions and false doctrines. He worships sticks and stones and all manner of external powers. We have countless sects, creeds, dogmas, opinions, and beliefs.

Making four parts of the garment is symbolic of the world as *four* means the created, manifested world of phenomena which we see. The *soldiers* symbolize warfare which is always within the unillumined and unregenerate mind of man. Man wages war over the letter of the Law and lacks the spirit of love which giveth life to all things good. We should act from the standpoint of love and the good; then there would be no bickering over differences in religion.

The coat was without seam, woven from the top throughout. This refers to the Infinite One which clothes all of us. We are all garments which God wears as He moves through the illusion of time and space. The Infinite is One and Indivisible. There could not be two powers because one would cancel out the other, and we would have a chaos instead of a cosmos. It is a mathematical impossibility to have two Infinites. You cannot multiply or divide Infinity.

In verse twenty-four we are told they cast lots for it. Man believes in a world of chance, coincidence, accident, bad luck, misfortune, etc. There is no chance in a world by law and order.

(28) *After this, Jesus knowing that all things were now accomplished, that the scripture might be fulfilled, saith, I thirst. (29) Now there was set a vessel full of vinegar: and they filled a sponge with vinegar, and put it upon hyssop, and put it to his mouth.*

I thirst refers to your intense desire to drink deep draughts of inner peace, satisfaction, and strength of the Holy One. I am sure you are now thirsting for your supreme ideal at this moment. Let God's river of peace move over the arid areas of your mind; this is the dew of heaven. You will begin to secrete the perfume from On High; a wonderful feeling of exaltation will follow; whatever is troubling you will be dissolved by the Radiance of the Light Limitless within you.

The sponge dipped in vinegar and put upon hyssop is, of course, purely symbolic and refers to a cleansing process of the mind. The cleansing properties of the plant, hyssop, are traditional in the East. "And the vinegar which was handed to Him seems to me to have been a symbolic thing . . . the reed signified the royal sceptre and the divine law." (Dionysius, Bp. of Alexandria, An Interpretation of Luke).

Sour wine mixed with myrrh was given in the East to refresh a thirsty person. This represents a transitional process whereby man forsakes all the false beliefs in the world and is resurrected mentally to a new concept of God and His Law.

In verse thirty the phrase, *It is finished,* means Amen, the answered prayer, or the silent, inner knowing of the soul. It is finished whenever there is nothing in our conscious or subconscious mind that challenges our conviction. The ultimate meaning of, *It is finished,* is that man has fully awakened from his dream of limitation here. He is the solid which has reached its melting point and has melted into the Boundless One.

The question is frequently asked, "Why did Jesus say on the cross, Eli, Eli, lama sabachthani?'" translated in this chapter as, "My God, my God, why hast thou forsaken me?" In the apocryphal Gospel of Peter, the dying Christ cries, "My power, thou hast forsaken me," which is different. The Encyclopedia Biblica says the original reading was presumably altered by scribes who only understood Syriac. The Aramaic word *sabachthani* means to keep, to preserve.

When a boy I asked a teacher this question, "How could Jesus have questioned God after knowing and proving the axiom, 'I and the Father are one.'"

You probably guess the reply. It was the old one, "Don't ask foolish questions."

The twenty second Psalm was quoted by Jesus, but the interpreter made an error in its translation from Hebrew and Aramaic. The word *sabachthani* in Hebrew means to glorify not to forsake, for which the word azabthani should have been used. The real meaning is, "My God, my God, how thou hast glorified me." *Shabach* root of *Sabachthani* means to glorify (Strong's *Concordance*).

Another translation which we gave you from the apocryphal scriptures, "My power, my power, thou hast forsaken me." *To forsake* is to relinquish, to release, to loosen, to be free from. The spiritual man forsakes the power of the world's beliefs and of things external and he gives all glory and honor to God— the One Supreme Power. He knows no other. In this sense his human will power is forsaken or given up completely, and man is now obedient to the One Will and is under Holy Orders* to bring forth the order, beauty, wholeness, perfection, and light of God here and now. This drama deals with the birth of the God-man in you.

(34) *But one of the soldiers with a spear pierced his side, and forthwith came there out blood and water.*

(36) *For these things were done, that the scripture should be fulfilled, A bone of him shall not be broken.*

The Encyclopedia Biblica points out the impossibility of explaining the issuing of blood and water from an internal source physiologically. In other words *blood and water* do not flow from a dead man; that is absurd. The terms *the water and the blood* are technical expressions for channels of Divine Grace (Love and Wisdom). A woman at birth releases blood and water. The symbolic significance refers to the spiritual rebirth or Cosmic Consciousness.

The statement about *a bone not being broken* signifies that Life is One and Indivisible, and denotes man's sense of oneness with the Living Spirit Almighty. *Not a bone (idea) is broken* means that we have no sense of separation, but we have a complete sense of fulness or at-one-ment with He Who Forever Is. We must have no distorted mental picture, but maintain

---

* See the chapter "Holy Orders" in my book *Prayer is the Answer.*

always a sense of wholeness, completion, and perfection; then not a bone of our body or consciousness will be broken.

The crucifixion in a mystical sense is God or the Absolute becoming man. The Limitless One crosses over from the Absolute State to the relative state. The Unconditional One becomes conditioned. The Formless One limits Himself by taking on shape, size, and dimension. Every new born babe is God becoming that child and in the depths of the subjective mind of the child is the Presence of God in all His glory. We are here to resurrect the God-Power within us and remove all obstacles and opposition, proving our divinity.

The crucifixion of Christ, according to the *Dictionary of the Sacred language of all Scriptures,* is a symbol of the Divine sacrifice; that is, the limitation and involution of the Divine energies and qualities within forms of matter. In other words God gives life to all of us and all things. God is involved in you and the whole redemptive process consists in evolving what is involved within you. As you release your Divine powers and qualities through increased knowledge and understanding, you become the conqueror over all fears, doubts, and false concepts. As you ascend spiritually, you will finally sense your oneness with He Who Is. You will become the God-man and do all the things which a son of God can do. You will unstop the ears of the deaf and open the eyes of the blind. You will glorify God every moment of your life.

Paul said, "I am crucified with Christ, nevertheless I live." How could anyone take this literally? He means he has crossed over into the Light. The word *Christ* means the Presence and Power of God functioning in your life. When you are illumined by the Light of God, you are crucified with Christ.

The Lord said unto John, Thou hearest that I suffered, yet I suffered not; that I was pierced, yet was I not smitten! that I was hanged, yet was I not hanged. See thou therefore in me the slaying of a word (Logos). Acts of John, second century.

How could God suffer? How could God be slain? How could God be wounded? Surely, it must be the illusion of pain and suffering. It is the slaying of a word. God seems to be slain and dead in us until we awaken from our slumber and hypnotic trance.

Is God asleep in your boat? You are the ship and when the storms of life appear, do not get excited. God is there. So, wake Him up! "Awake thou that sleepest and rise from the dead, and Christ will give thee light."

In verse thirty-eight of this chapter it says that *Joseph of Arimathaea* took away the body of Jesus. Joseph of Aramathaea means a high disciplined imagination or a high state of consciousness. Our ideal must be *entombed in a sepulchre* which signifies a deep, subjective embodiment, a tomb-like state where we place our concept. A *stone* (conviction) seals the tomb. This is where we place Jesus, our new ideal. The past is dead, forgotten, and remembered no more. Behold! I make all things new!

Chapter 20

(1) *The first day of the week cometh Mary Magdalene early, when it was yet dark, unto the sepulchre, and seeth the stone taken away from the sepulchre. (2) Then she runneth, and cometh to Simon Peter, and to the other disciple, whom Jesus loved, and saith unto them, They have taken away the Lord out of the sepulchre, and we know not where they have laid him. (3) Peter therefore went forth, and that other disciple, and came to the sepulchre. (4) So they ran both together: and the other disciple did outrun Peter, and came first to the sepulchre. (5) And he stooping down, and looking in, saw the linen clothes lying; yet went he not in. (6) Then cometh Simon Peter following him, and went into the sepulchre, and seeth the linen clothes lie, (7) And the napkin, that was about his head, not lying with the linen clothes, but wrapped together in a place by itself. (8) Then went in also that other disciple, which came first to the sepulchre, and he saw, and believed. (9) For as yet they knew not the scripture, that he must rise again from the dead.*

(10) Then the disciples went away again unto their own home.

Mary Magdalene signifies love redeemed. The publican and the harlot are ofttimes the first to see the truth. The harlot has hit the depths of degradation and is free of all false pride, egotism, and is very conscious of her own insufficiency. When she hungers and thirsts after the truth, she receives it because she has created a vacuum in her mind which receives the soft tread of the Unseen Guest. She then comes under Holy Orders. She trusts the Infinite to lead, guide, and direct her without dictating or outlining the way. She knows the way of God is good and very good. The Infinite Love and Grace of God plus the movement of the Law take her out of her misery and bring light and peace into her heart.

The stone taken away from the sepulchre represents the new attitude of mind, an awareness of the Spiritual Power which rolls away the stone of false beliefs. The real meaning of the *resurrection of Christ* is to raise up health, peace, joy, and happiness from your own depths. Man's belief is the sepulchre in which his health, wisdom, and peace are confined. Man's

opinions and false ideas are the psychological garments which he wears. The new interpretation of
life—a new mental attitude—is the *angel* which rolls
away the stone. Man's awakening to the Power of God
bursts the bands of his creed and fears and he rises
from his dead beliefs to the truth which sets him free.
He walks without his crutches; this is the resurrection
of Christ or health. The resurrection from the dead
is taking place every hour of the day in many parts of
the world.

The *disciples* in this chapter mean our faculties of
mind, our mental attitudes. *Jesus seen by the disciples*
means Jesus (your desire) is rising—our concept rises
from the subjective to the conscious mind.

In verse seven *the napkin that was about his head*
means the revealing of the new state. If your face is
covered, I don't recognize you. When man unclothes
himself psychologically, he finds God. The Reality
of You is Mind, Spirit. You are the house of God and
whatever you pray for already is in the Kingdom of
Reality within you. Remove the napkin, i.e., shut out
of the senses anything which denies your good, and
rejoice in the reality of your desire in your consciousness, and it shall come to pass. Discard the old and put
on the new!

(11) *But Mary stood without at the sepulchre weep-
ing: and as she wept, she stooped down, and looked into*

the sepulchre, (12) And seeth two angels in white sitting, the one at the head, and the other at the feet, where the body of Jesus had lain.

The two angels sitting at the tomb represent the present state of peace and a new desire. When our prayer is answered, we are satisfied for the time being, but immediately another desire to further transcend takes place.

(19) Then the same day at evening, being the first day of the week, when the doors were shut where the disciples were assembled for fear of the Jews, came Jesus and stood in the midst, and saith unto them, Peace be unto you,

Jesus appearing to his disciples and speaking to them means that we discipline or speak to our faculties of mind (or concept), and we become poised in the truth. Jesus—representing the solution or the answered prayer—is now made manifest, and the faculties of mind are aware of the fact. When the solution comes, it whispers, "Peace be unto you."

(20) And when he had so said, he shewed unto them his hands, and his side. Then were the disciples glad, when they saw the Lord.

This means that all our faculties rejoice in the answered prayer. We bubble over with joyous enthusiasm. Your yearning and hungering is now satisfied, at least temporarily. The new state of mind always establishes its objective counterpart and unification.

(22) He breathed on them, and saith unto them, Receive ye the Holy Ghost.

Breath symbolizes life. We receive the Holy Ghost (whole spirit) when we are integrated and no longer divided in our mind. Now our spirit (feeling) is one with our desire; we are again whole, united, and at peace. Man with a desire is dual; man, one with his ideal or desire, has received the Holy Ghost or feeling of wholeness or oneness with his aim in life. He achieves the state of wholeness or unity by breathing the breath of the life into his idea, and lives, moves, and has his being in that mental atmosphere.

(24) But Thomas, one of the twelve, called Didymus, was not with them when Jesus came. (25) The other disciples therefore said unto him, We have seen the Lord. But he said unto them, Except I shall see in his hands the print of the nails, and put my finger into the print of the nails, and thrust my hand into his side, I will not believe.

Thomas was called the doubter, the faculty in you when disciplined which challenges every rumor that questions the Truths of God. *He thrusts his hand into the side* means he touches reality and only accepts the divine solution. This is why it is said that he, alone of all the disciples, puts his *finger into the print of the nails and touched Jesus,* or the solution.

Chapter 21

(1) After these things Jesus shewed himself again to the disciples at the sea of Tiberias; and on this wise shewed he himself. (2) There were together Simon Peter, and Thomas called Didymus, and Nathanael of Cana in Galilee, and the sons of Zebedee, and two other of his disciples. (3) Simon Peter saith unto them, I go a fishing. They say unto him, We also go with thee. They went forth, and entered into a ship immediately; and that night they caught nothing. (4) But when the morning was now come, Jesus stood on the shore: but the disciples knew not that it was Jesus, (5) Then Jesus saith unto them, Children, have ye any meat? They answered him, No. (6) And he said unto them, Cast the net on the right side of the ship, and ye shall find. They cast therefore, and now they were not able to draw it for the multitude of fishes. (7) Therefore that disciple whom Jesus loved saith unto Peter, It is the Lord. Now when Simon Peter heard that it was the Lord, he girt his fisher's coat unto him (for he was naked,) and did cast himself into the sea.

(8) And the other disciples came in a little ship; (for they were not far from land, but as it were two hundred cubits,) dragging the net with fishes. (9) As soon then as they were come to land, they saw a fire of coals there, and fish laid thereon, and bread. (10) Jesus saith unto them, Bring of the fish which ye have now caught. (11) Simon Peter went up, and drew the net to land full of great fishes, an hundred and fifty and three: and for all there were so many, yet was not the net broken. (12) Jesus saith unto them, Come and dine, And none of the disciples durst ask him, Who art thou? knowing that it was the Lord.

This is a story of fishing. We are all fishermen because we are endeavoring to fish out of the depths of ourselves all the answers to our problems. The *fishermen* are states of mind within ourselves, faculties, and attitudes of mind. *The ship we enter* is, of course, our own mind inasmuch as we are always traveling in our mind. The moment we have a problem, we begin to move psychologically trying to solve it. We begin to look for the solution, the way out; this is called fishing in the Bible.

Here is how Einstein fished many ideas out of the depths of his subliminal mind. He knew the answers to his problems were within. He stilled the conscious mind, thought about the answer from all angles, listening quietly for any bit of guidance that would come, joining all the threads together, and ofttimes the whole answer would come into his mind. At other times after thinking quietly and with interest on the answer to his problem, he would turn it over to his Deeper Mind with faith and confidence, knowing that the Infinite Intelligence within would give him the answer. This he called the incubation process. The subconscious seemed to take his request, dwell on it for awhile, and when it had assembled all the facts presented them to his conscious mind. The surface mind when it is still receives wisdom, guidance, and answers to problems from the Deeper Mind. These answers pop into the mind like toast out of a toaster.

The other night a friend of mine, a local minister, lost a very important document. I stilled my mind by recalling the truths of the 91st Psalm and imagined he was telling me he found it. I heard his voice over and over again; shortly my subjective self whispered in my ear, "His brother-in-law's car." This is called true clairaudience, i.e., where you actually hear the Subjective Wisdom speak to you. Its thoughts become audible only to the ear which is attuned; others in the room do not hear it. You can hear the answer to anything and fish it out of your subjective depths if you get still and know the answer is there; then listen for it—lowly listening is the answer. This minister, at my suggestion, phoned his brother-in-law; the latter was amazed to find the document under a rug in his car. He does not know how it got there, but the Subjective Wisdom knew how it got there and where the paper was.

Many people fish all night, i.e., in the night of human darkness and ignorance of the laws of mind, not knowing where the Source of all their good is. There is a right and a wrong way to do everything.

For example, there is a right and a wrong way to bake a cake, to write a letter, to make a speech. There is a right and a wrong way to think and to live. If you do not learn how to think (fish) constructively and cooperate with mental and spiritual laws, you will get into a lot of trouble. If you have the wrong attitude toward life, everything will seem to go wrong.

I knew a girl who hated another. She had a grudge attitude. Through explanation she learned to fish out love, good will, and kindness toward the other by praying for the girl she hated. She prayed for the girl's guidance, happiness, and peace by sincerely wishing all these things for her. She did this frequently. They became the best of friends. The sequel was that she married the girl's brother whom she formerly resented. This is fishing on the right side. Your mind is the net receiving all kinds of fish; i.e., thoughts, feelings, psychic patterns, hopes, fears, intrigues, etc. of the race mind.

The universal subjectivity or collective unconscious of the race impinges itself on all of us. We are immersed in the great sea of mind. Ofttimes you wonder at the weird thoughts that wander into your mind. Chop the head off these negative, destructive thoughts that swim up to your surface mind, kill them, cremate them with the fire of Divine Love, true concepts, and constructive imagery. Think right, do right, feel right, act right, be right, and keep up fishing on the right side of the ship. Reject all negative intrusions into your mental household. Look over the net (your mind); see if there are any rotten fish; throw them out; consume them with the fire of true, scientific thinking! Do this incisively and decisively, and you will be a good fisherman.

In verse four the solution is always at hand. Truth is Omnipresent; so it is said that they *knew not it was Jesus*. They had not yet recognized the Truth.

In verse six the command to *cast the net on the right side of the ship* means the right use of the Law for the solution to our problem. Having cast their nets (their ideas or desire) in the subjective—and since God always giveth the increase—they were answered with a multitude of fishes; this means the Divine measure or good multiplied. The subconscious always multiplies exceedingly and gives compound interest on whatever deposits we make there.

In verse seven *Peter* symbolizes faith. Peter *casting himself into the sea* means that when our consciousness is disciplined so that we believe implicitly in our good, everything will succeed.

In verse nine *land* is manifestation. The *fire of coals* is the fire of illumination, the warmth of the Spirit, and the feeling of security. *The fish* are always there, signifying that out of the moods of peace and harmony come all the things we would feed on in this world.

In verse eleven one hundred and fifty-three fish were caught. One, plus five, plus three adds up to nine. In nine months a woman gives birth to a child, so it means when we fish aright, we will always be impregnated with our desire. Nine is a symbol of possession and mastery. The old adage is that possession is nine points; following our feeling of possession comes the manifestation which is called ten or our good objectified. When your friend tells you that you can't achieve, that your desire is impossible to attain, go within and fish the mood of faith and confidence in God out of your depths, and you will also draw its manifestations or experiences. It is wonderful!

The following are some highlights of key verses: (15) *So when they had dined, Jesus saith to Simon Peter, Simon, son of Jonas, lovest thou me more than these? He saith unto him, Yea, Lord; thou knowest that I love thee. He saith unto him, Feed my lambs.*

Lambs are tended animals—moods that will bless us. Feed my lambs means that we must feed these things we want, think feelingly of them.

(18) *Verily, verily, I say unto thee, When thou wast young, thou girdest thyself, and walkedst whither thou wouldest: but when thou shalt be old, thou shalt stretch forth thy hands, and another shall gird thee, and carry thee whither thou wouldest not.*

This verse means that when we are young in the Truth, our faith is not always strong. We sometimes act without thinking and do just as we please. When we are old, we stretch forth our hand; we have more power and more understanding. We are more firmly anchored; this faith or mental attitude will carry us further.

(22) *Jesus saith unto him, If I will that he tarry till I come, what is that to thee? follow thou me.*

This verse refers to mystical creation. It symbolizes John or love. We must love our ideal; then Jesus—or the solution—comes. This verse also teaches us a wonderful lesson in minding our own business. People oftentimes will say, "What about the Jones next door? They rob, cheat, and defraud; yet they seem to prosper?" A man can have a million dollars and be poor in peace, harmony, love, and health. He cannot buy them.

(25) *And there are also many other things which Jesus did, the which, if they should be written every one, I suppose that even the world itself could not contain the books that should be written. Amen.*

Verse twenty-five tells all of us that here the mystic is not referring to the man Jesus, but to the dramatizations of I AM or God. God thinks, and worlds appear. The whole cosmos is God thinking. There is not room in this small world of ours to contain the works of the Infinite One. What volume or volumes would record the deeds of the Infinite?

All men shall see the Light. When man awakens to his True Self, he will experience the radiance of the Light Limitless. From the field of sin and punishment, he shall pass into the boundless freedom of the divine perfection. Let us realize the truth of the following verse from Arnold:

"Never the spirit shall die,
The spirit shall cease to be never.
Never the spirit was not.
End and beginning are dreams.

Birthless and deathless and changeless—
Remaineth the spirit forever.
Death hath not changed it at all.
Dead though the house of it seems."

About the Author

A native of Ireland who resettled in America, Joseph Murphy, Ph.D., D.D. (1898–1981) was a prolific and widely admired New Thought minister and writer, best known for his metaphysical classic, *The Power of Your Subconscious Mind*, an international bestseller since it first appeared on the self-help scene in 1963. A popular speaker, Murphy lectured on both American coasts and in Europe, Asia, and South Africa. His many books and pamphlets on the auto-suggestive and metaphysical faculties of the human mind have entered multiple editions—some of the most poignant of which appear in this volume. Murphy is considered one of the pioneering voices of affirmative-thinking philosophy.